OECD Public Governance Reviews

Innovation Skills in the Public Sector

BUILDING CAPABILITIES IN CHILE

This work is published under the responsibility of the Secretary-General of the OECD. The opinions expressed and arguments employed herein do not necessarily reflect the official views of OECD member countries.

This document and any map included herein are without prejudice to the status of or sovereignty over any territory, to the delimitation of international frontiers and boundaries and to the name of any territory, city or area.

Please cite this publication as:
OECD (2017), *Innovation Skills in the Public Sector: Building Capabilities in Chile*, OECD Public Governance Reviews, OECD Publishing, Paris.
http://dx.doi.org/10.1787/9789264273283-en

ISBN 978-92-64-27327-6 (print)
ISBN 978-92-64-27328-3 (PDF)

Series: OECD Public Governance Reviews
ISSN 2219-0406 (print)
ISSN 2219-0414 (online)

The statistical data for Israel are supplied by and under the responsibility of the relevant Israeli authorities. The use of such data by the OECD is without prejudice to the status of the Golan Heights, East Jerusalem and Israeli settlements in the West Bank under the terms of international law.

Photo credits: Cover Ministerio Secretaria General de Gobierno. Licenced under a Creative Commons Attribution-ShareAlike (CC BY 2.0)

Corrigenda to OECD publications may be found on line at: *www.oecd.org/about/publishing/corrigenda.htm*.

Foreword

The Government of Chile has set out a vision to develop a more inclusive society, and sees public sector innovation as a means to achieve it. Chile's efforts to change and improve the public sector are not new, but rather part of a long tradition of reform and modernisation that began in the 1990s. To this end, Chile has created the *Laboratorio de Gobierno*, a multidisciplinary government institution that develops, facilitates and promotes innovation processes within public sector institutions.

The Chilean Government asked the OECD to review the innovation-related skills and capabilities of the Chilean public service and identify ways to support and improve them. This is the first such study to be carried out in an OECD country. It is guided by a theoretical framework developed with Chilean public servants that looks at the abilities, motivations and opportunities in the public service for contributing to innovation.

The study shows that enhancing the Chilean state's capacity for innovation will require a system-wide approach and a co-ordinated effort across multiple institutions. Success will also greatly depend on effective leadership in every public organisation. Building a skilled workforce through better recruitment and development is a start, but there is also a need for tools to motivate innovation as well as leadership that understands how to provide opportunities to put these skills and motivations to work.

This report provides recommendations on how to further develop a common vision and understanding of public sector innovation, and how to align this vision with the activities of the organisations responsible for implementing it. The recommendations focus primarily on the *Laboratorio de Gobierno*, whose primary mission is to embed innovation in the Chilean public sector, and on the National Civil Service Directorate, which provides central guidance and oversight on human resource management (HRM) issues in the public sector and manages the Senior Executive System. The role of *Laboratorio* will shift in coming years as it takes on different functions, and its structure and governance may need to adapt to these changes. The National Department of Civil Service should also use its influence to promote innovation in agencies, in particular through their HRM and workforce development.

The report builds on previous work carried out by the OECD Observatory for Public Sector Innovation (OPSI) and the Public Employment and Management Working Party (PEM). The Abilities, Motivation and Opportunities framework that guides the report was first discussed with the PEM and resulted in the chapter on HRM in the OECD report, *Fostering Innovation in the Public Sector*. This report also draws on the 2016 Survey on Strategic Human Resource Management in Central/Federal Governments of OECD Countries, conducted by the PEM. This survey included, for the first time, a set of comparative data on the use of tools to support public innovation. Furthermore, the report presents multiple case studies and examples collected from OECD countries through the OPSI online platform, the OPSI National Points of Contact network, and the PEM. The review benefited from discussions at the Future State conference organised jointly by the OECD and the Government of Chile in March 2016 in Santiago, as well as comments from the OPSI NCP and the PEM working party.

ACKNOWLEDGEMENTS

This review was prepared by the Public Governance and Territorial Development Directorate of the OECD. The mission of the Public Governance and Territorial Development Directorate is to help governments at all levels design and implement strategic, evidence-based and innovative policies to strengthen public governance, respond effectively to diverse and disruptive economic, social and environmental challenges and deliver on government's commitments to citizens.

The report was prepared by Marco Daglio, in charge of the Public Governance and Territorial Development's work on public sector innovation, and Daniel Gerson, in charge of the Public Governance and Territorial Development's work on Public Employment and Management. Strategic directions were provided by Edwin Lau, Head of the Public Sector Reform Division, and Luiz de Mello, Deputy Director of the Public Governance and Territorial Development Directorate.

Chapters 1 - 4 were drafted by Laura Skoratko, and Cristina Mendes, (OECD Secretariat, Reform of the Public Sector Division). The full report benefited from contributions and revisions provided by Daniel Gerson and Marco Daglio. Marie-Claude Gohier helped with the preparation of the final publication. Bettina Huggard and Susan Rantalainen provided administrative support and assisted with the logistics related to the data collection.

National peer reviewers from France and the USA provided very valuable contributions and orientation to the review. For France, Francoise Waintrop of the Prime Minister's Secretariat-General for Modernisation of Public Action. For USA, Megan Lazier from the Innovation Lab at the Office of Personnel Management of the Federal Government.

The review team wishes to acknowledge the contributions provided by over 300 Chilean stakeholders from the public, social and private sector during interviews and in answering the OECD surveys that were administered for the purpose of this review.

Finally, this review would not have been possible without the commitment and support of the *Laboratorio de Gobierno*, its open and committed staff members, and the members of its board of directors.

We are particularly thankful to Juan Felipe López, Executive Director of the *Laboratorio*, Gianncarlo Durán, Director of the Skills programme and Rodrigo Egana, Head of the National Department of Civil Service for their insights and support along the review process.

Table of contents

Figures

Tables

Boxes

Executive Summary

Chile's use of innovation to improve its public sector is part of a long tradition of modernisation started in the early 1990s and includes the creation of *Servicio de Impuestos Internos* online, *ChileCompra* and *Chile Atiende*. This report examines how civil servants in Chile contribute to innovation in the public sector, providing insight into the challenges they face and what can be done to strengthen their capacity to innovate in Chile's public sector.

Abilities: Strengthening central guidance to ensure a coherent approach to skills development

In order to innovate, Chilean civil servants require specific technical skills and knowledge as well as a range of "softer" behavioural and cognitive skills such as creative thinking and communication. Such abilities are found in Chile's public services, but in pockets that are not well developed or supported institutionally. Particular gaps may exist in skills related to working with citizens and with iterative innovation projects.

Abilities, once defined and understood, need to be incorporated into an organisation, either through recruitment or through the development of existing employees. The *Laboratorio de Gobierno* has begun to address some of these skills gaps through *Experimenta*, a development programme that takes a "learn-by-doing" approach to build innovation capabilities in 12 public institutions each year. The programme is designed around solid concepts of experiential learning and coaching, but will take time to produce measurable results.

To complement this initiative, **standards and guidance should be established by central authorities such as the National Directorate for Civil Service (DNSC) and the *Laboratorio* to support a more coherent development of innovation skills**. This includes updating existing guidelines for recruitment managers, designing opportunities to share good practices amongst hiring and training authorities of public organisations and designing tools that could encourage mobility and internships as a way of developing staff, spreading ideas, and sharing hard-to-find skill sets across organisations.

Motivation: Creating incentives and fostering a culture of innovation

To motivate civil servants to innovate, organisations must value innovation and reward the associated behaviour. The Chilean civil servants who participated in the project demonstrated a very high level of motivation to contribute to innovation and to improve the services they deliver to citizens. Often, however, this motivation is dampened by a bureaucracy that is perceived as rigid and organisational cultures that favour compliance over creative problem solving. **Employee surveys should be used to assess organisational culture, benchmark employee perceptions and build an evidence base that can help guide and improve innovation-oriented management practices.**

Awards and networks can also help to connect and motivate successful and future innovators. Chile's *Functiona!* awards and the nascent Public Innovators Network are beginning to unearth and reward successful innovation, and link innovators across Chile's public services. **The impact of awards and networks should be expanded by, for example, further developing the shortlisted innovations into case studies and making them available to the network and others in order to encourage replication.**

Opportunity: Supporting leaders to encourage innovation

Highly capable and motivated public sector innovators will only achieve real innovation if they are given opportunities to put those skills and motivation to work. Employees need a certain amount of autonomy to contribute to innovation. Chilean public employees perceive few opportunities to put their innovation skills into practice. Many spoke of the need for more resources, time, training, management and leadership approaches to create spaces for innovation.

Leadership and good management are crucial for supporting a more innovative public sector, however not all public leaders or managers appear to have a common understanding of what innovation means in the context of Chile's public sector. **A shared vision and agenda for public sector innovation, developed through broad consultation exercises with Chilean public employees, would help to create a common understanding of what innovation is trying to accomplish in Chile's public sector.** Leaders can then align resources and activities to support this vision, creating safe places (e.g. labs, innovation units) to experiment and test new ideas. Middle managers have a direct role to set team expectations, provide support and give permission to try new things.

Given the central role for Chile's public management community, little is done to define and develop innovation-oriented leaders and managers. **Defining innovation as a competency would help clarify the kinds of leadership and management behaviours expected of innovative public managers in Chile's public sector**. These can then be included in development material, performance management and promotion regimes. While the Senior Executive System can provide an entry point for these kinds of intervention at the top two levels of the hierarchy, middle management levels should also be included in innovation-oriented development activities.

Fostering innovation skills in Chile's public sector

Building public sector innovation capabilities involves complex interrelations among many institutional actors and systems, ranging from recruitment to development of civil servants, from innovation awards to networks of innovators, from strengthening a collaborative organisational culture to developing the capacity to lead innovation. As such, fostering innovation requires developing parallel and complementary approaches by different actors. In Chile these include:

- **The *Laboratorio***, a new organisation in the Chilean public service, contributes fresh insight and expertise and has opened up a space for controlled experimentation and collaboration within government. Over the course of the next years, the role of the *Laboratorio* will shift as it takes on new and different functions, and this will need to be matched by ongoing monitoring of its achievements, and consideration of its structure and governance.

- **The National Department of the Civil Service** will also need to make the most of the recent legislation that expands opportunities to support agencies in their human resource management and workforce development and be a driving force in promoting cross-government tools and awards to encourage innovation.
- **Every public leader and manager** has a role to play in ensuring that his or her own public institution is equipped with a workforce that possess the skills, motivation and opportunities to contribute to innovation that will improve the lives of Chileans across the country.

Chapter 1.

Workforce capabilities for innovation in the Chilean public sector

This chapter provides an overview of the theoretical framework used to assess innovation skills and capabilities in Chile's public sector and maps the institutional landscape for public sector innovation and human resource management. The analytical framework identifies three elements that public employees in Chile require: abilities, motivations and opportunities to contribute to innovation in their public organisations. Chile's interest in building innovation capabilities in its public sector builds on decades of public sector modernisation initiatives. However, the complexity of governance challenges and low citizen trust in government institutions calls for new approaches to policy making and service delivery. The Laboratorio de Gobierno, along with the National Civil Service Directorate, are two important institutions with the potential to contribute to a more innovative Chilean public sector.

Why human resources management is important for innovation

Governments around the world are operating in a new landscape which requires new approaches to the complex challenges they face. Public sector innovation can be defined as implementing something new in the context of a public sector institution to address a public policy challenge that achieves results of value for society. Governments have always innovated both the way the work and the services they provide – yet there is no formal established guidance to get the conditions right for generating innovation in the public sector. Many OECD governments are experimenting with a range of tools and interventions to encourage and support innovation in their public sectors; however the ability to measure their effectiveness depends on a variety of contextual factors both at individual, organisational and societal level. In many cases it is still too early to declare success.

Many of these interventions focus on public employees. People are at the core of public sector innovation. Ideas for new services and business activities are sparked in the minds of civil servants, political leaders, service users and members of the broader community, and are developed and brought to scale through the dedication of a wide variety of professionals and stakeholders at different stages of the process. Research on public sector innovations suggests innovative ideas are often initiated by middle managers or frontline staff (Borins, 2014, Hartley, 2006). When supported and motivated, frontline staff and middle managers can play an active role in bringing forward innovative ideas and working them through every stage of the process.

People management is therefore an important lever for sustaining public sector innovation and has been identified as one key area where countries should focus efforts to raise their innovative potential (see annex 1.A). Furthermore, promoting innovation within the workforce is a top priority for HRM reform in OECD countries.[1] Factors that are expected to have an impact include communication networks, rewards and incentive structures, managerial and leadership styles, organisational practices related to the attraction, selection, training and compensation of employees, and job design factors such as the use of teams and delegation of decision-making rights. However, underlying causal mechanisms are still being explored and are not fully understood.

Purpose and Methodology of the Study

This study is the first of its kind, looking at the use of HR tools for civil service capacity building with a specific focus on public sector innovation in an OECD country. The government of Chile has shown great leadership in working with the OECD to undertake this study, and advance knowledge in this nascent field of research. Consequently, it has been exploratory in nature; guided by a theoretical framework and structured in a way that allows each step to build on the knowledge developed in the previous phase.

Box 1.1. Research phases

Given that this is the first review of this kind, the OECD and the Government of Chile worked together to develop an exploratory research process that puts Chilean civil servants and innovators' experience at the centre. Each step of the process built on the findings of the previous one.

1. Development of a theoretical framework: the OECD, with input from the *Laboratorio de Gobierno* and its board of directors, developed the framework based on previous research conducted by the OECD on the abilities, motivations and opportunities of civil servants to innovate.
2. A survey with open questions, based on the framework, was developed and completed by the *Laboratorio* and other stakeholders in order to collect initial data and evidence that would give the OECD team a broad and basic understanding of governance and innovation in Chile. This was complemented by Chile's completion of the 2016 Strategic Human Resources Survey in early 2016, together with all other OECD countries.
3. A first mission (November 2015) was held to get a contextual overview of the innovation landscape: in Chile's public sector, providing deeper and more nuanced insights than the initial survey could allow. This included interviews and focus group discussions with over 100 key public employees, senior leaders, academics, and members of civil society in order to understand the current context of innovation in the Chilean public sector. This mission included peers from the Prime Minister's office in France and the Office of Personnel Management's Innovation Lab in the USA.
4. A second mission (March 2016) was held to conduct a series of workshops with Chilean public sector innovators, managers of innovation projects, and senior leaders. These interactive workshops were designed around project lifecycles to explore the range of skills and competencies used by Chileans in their innovation processes, as well as the perceived gaps in their skills sets and barriers overcome along the way. This mission included participation in an international conference of public sector innovators where workshops were offered in partnership with Nesta, the UK's innovation charity.
5. A third mission (November 2016) offered the OECD an opportunity to engage again with groups of key stakeholders to present an assessment developed from the outcomes of the first two missions and to test areas of recommendations. Comparisons with OECD's database of country practices. This mission included an opportunity to pilot a survey tool which enables identification of perceived individual skills gaps, management capacity and organisational readiness (Box 2.3).

The framework that guides the study is based on research previously conducted with the OECD's working party on Public Employment and Management. It builds on an established theory of employee behaviour which states that civil servants and employees of any organisation will perform when they have the **Abilities**, **Motivation** and **Opportunities** to contribute to their organisation's goals (Boxall and Purcell, 2011). This means that teaching skills for innovation alone will not boost the innovative capacity of a workforce without taking a wider systems-view of Chile's institutional structures (both supports and constraints) and workforce management.

The framework drives a systemic view, linking the skills and capacities of individual civil servants with the specific institutional features of the Chilean public sector to increase and improve public sector innovation:

- **Abilities to innovate**. Abilities are generally thought of in terms of skills, knowledge and, increasingly, behaviours that a person possesses. There is no agreed definition of innovation skills – particularly in the public sector – yet research and experience suggest that innovation skills can be considered in terms of hard skills (ability to use specific tools/technologies and methodologies) and soft skills (behaviours or orientations). After mapping which skills and knowledge contribute to innovation in the Chilean public sector, a key question would be: are these prevalent and how can such competencies be acquired, developed and nurtured?
- **Motivation to innovate**. While ability will determine what the workforce is capable of doing, motivation determines what the workforce will actually do: how can HRM practices influence employees to want to innovate? How can they be encouraged to do so by their organisations, managers and leaders? Motivating employees to contribute to innovation depends upon a careful balance of intrinsic and extrinsic motivational factors. Intrinsic motivation is discussed in relation to building innovation-friendly organisational cultures using management tools such as employee surveys. Looking at extrinsic motivators requires an institutional lens and a closer look at an organisation's incentives and rewards for innovation.
- **Opportunity to innovate**. This section looks at how leadership can help create space for innovation within public organisations and provide capable and motivated civil servants with the chance to innovate. This third element shifts the focus towards the organisational enablers for public sector innovation and the structures and strategies that organisations take to align resources with the objective to innovate. Specific institutional leadership and features of the public sector can increase the opportunity for public servants to innovate and create the space for public sector innovation.

This framework has been developed to examine how individual countries' HR systems support innovation. It has been applied here for the first time to examine innovation skills and institutional readiness for public sector innovation in Chile. This study provides an assessment of the HR system in Chile against its capacity to identify, sustain and develop the skills necessary for innovation, and provide recommendations on interventions that can support more and better public sector innovation in Chile. The study is based on data collected through interviews and workshops with over 150 Chilean civil servants and stakeholders, to understand the strengths and challenges of the capacity of the Chilean civil service to support innovation, including the skills and institutional enablers that are the most important to innovate in the Chilean public sector.

Given the ground-breaking nature of this study and the nascent degree of knowledge in this field, there is little comparable data available to benchmark the assessment of Chile against other OECD countries. Chile's leadership in undertaking this project has enabled the development and refining of a framework that can now be applied to other country systems to enable comparisons between Chile and other OECD countries around how to effectively develop effective HR systems and civil service capabilities to support innovation. Where possible, the review draws on OECD research on the enablers of innovation, country public governance reviews and on ongoing research in partnership with the European Commission and Nesta (the UK National Endowment for Science

Technology and the Arts) to establish a skills framework for public sector innovation. It also benefits from findings from past reviews of Chile and a number of OECD databases – both quantitative and qualitative – notably the Observatory for Public Sector Innovation Database as well as OECD data on public employment and civil service management systems, collected through the 2016 Strategic Human Resources Management survey.

This review offers concrete recommendations to support the goal of creating a more innovative Chilean public sector. They aim at supporting and advancing the *Laboratorio de Gobierno*'s ambition to be a catalyst for a wider systemic culture change across the Chilean civil service but also to go one step further to propose concrete actions in order to ensure that innovation is not only something confined to the laboratory, but is streamlined throughout Chile's public sector.

The review also provides the *Laboratorio*, the National Department of the Civil Service (DNSC) and senior leaders and managers with various comparative examples of other OECD countries who are equally engaging in efforts to enhance the innovation capacity of their public sectors and are, at times, facing similar challenges.

Innovation in the Chilean Public Sector: Vision and institutional context

Chile's efforts towards change and improvement in the public sector are not new but part of a long tradition of reform and modernisation efforts since the 1990s. These continued efforts have made the country a leader in Latin American for its effective and stable public governance and innovative solutions (e.g. Chile Atiende, a multiservice platform to connect citizens with a number of public services) (Figure 1.1).

Figure 1.1. Examples of key public sector modernisations in Chile

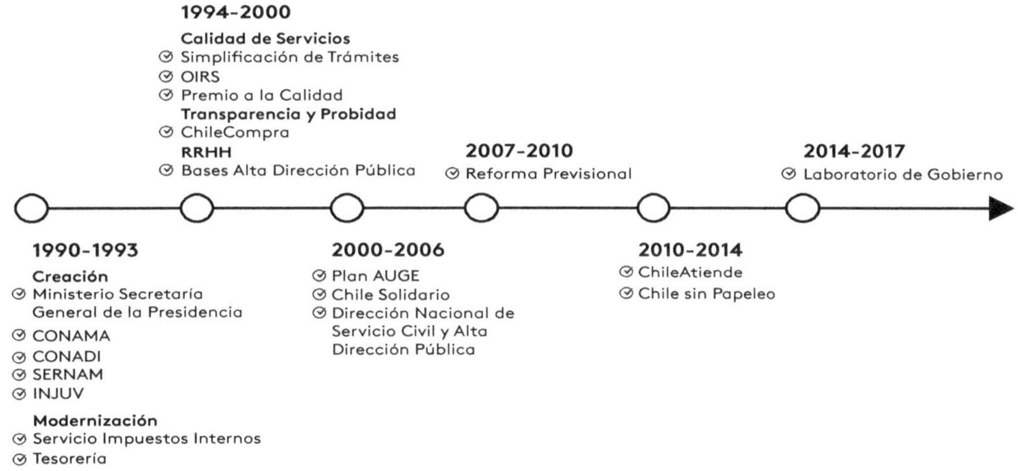

Source: Laboratorio de Gobierno.

This tradition of reform and change continues today in a context where the range and scale of the challenges Chile has to cope with have dramatically worsened in terms of trust and productivity. As in many OECD countries, Chile faces a crisis of trust between citizens and government. According to Gallup data, this level of trust has decreased

12 percentage points between 2007 and 2013 (Figure 1.2). The low level of public sector productivity requires governments to provide quality public services with the same or less resources. The increased complexity of policy challenges government have to face poses serious challenges to government action calling for new ways of approaching their solution based on active involvement and co-creation between service users, public servants and other actors, like entrepreneurs and academia.

Figure 1.2. Confidence in national government in 2012 and its change since 2007

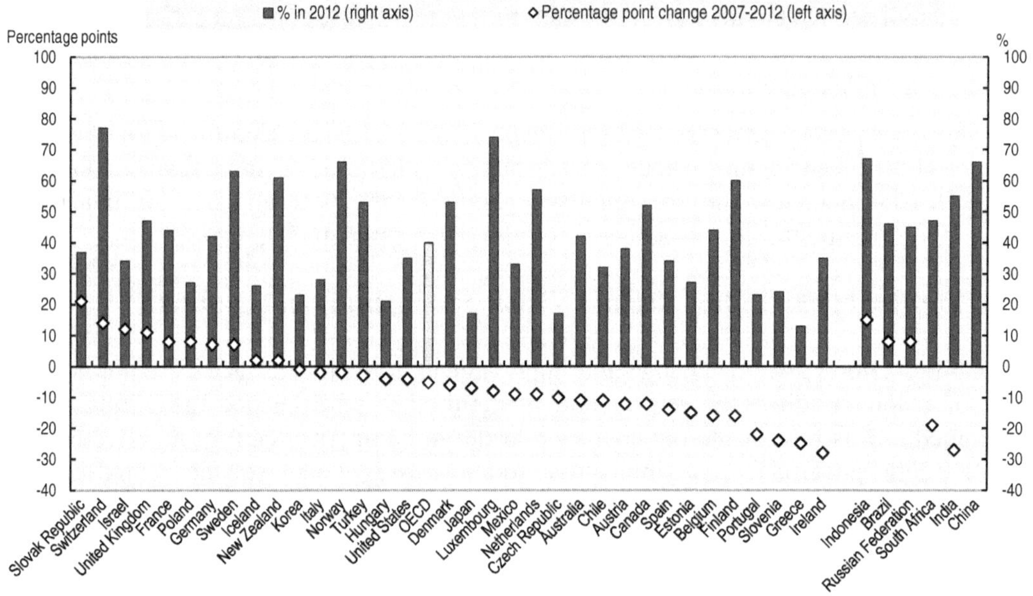

Statlink: http://dx.doi.org/10.1787/888932940740

Source: Gallup World Poll published in OECD Government at a Glance 2013.

The Government of Chile's vision is to develop a more inclusive society, and innovation is the means to achieve it. One key element of President Bachelet's programme is to "go beyond Modernization and reach an innovative State to rebuild the relationship between citizens and public institutions"[2] and rebuild the confidence of citizens in government. On the one hand, this includes reforming democratic institutions to increase transparency and raise standards of integrity and accountability. On the other hand, it includes constructing new policy areas and developing new approaches to involve civil society in the development, implementation and evaluation of public policies and services, to ensure they are providing public value.

The Laboratorio de Gobierno

The *Laboratorio de Gobierno* is a multidisciplinary institution of the Government of Chile which was set up to implement the President's mandate on public sector innovation. Announced by President Michelle Bachelet on 21 May 2014, the *Laboratorio* has the mission of developing, facilitating and promoting human-centred innovation processes within public sector institutions. The *Laboratorio* represents the Chilean Government's new approach to solving public challenges which put the citizens right in the centre of public action and transformation processes.

The *Laboratorio* acts as a learning-by-doing area for civil servants and provides a controlled environment that permits risk-taking and connects a diversity of actors related to public services to co-create and test solutions. The *Laboratorio* engages in two main streams of activity:

- **Innovation projects and ecosystem**: these include actions aimed supporting public sector institutions to seek innovative solutions that improve the services the State provides to citizens. This includes projects (such as open innovation challenges) with the objective to use the creative intelligence of entrepreneurs, small businesses, students, academics, citizens and NGOs to come up with solutions to the most urgent challenges of the State. Projects include the new redesign of the electricity bill, and projects in the healthcare sector, social welfare, transport and with the development agency CORFO.
- **Innovation capabilities**: these include actions focused on developing capabilities of civil servants to initiate and carry out innovation processes within public sector institutions through learning-by-doing experiences. Projects include *Experimenta* (experiential programme for civil servants discussed further in Chapter 2); and managing networks of innovations such as the *Innovadores Públicos*, the Public Innovators Network (discussed further in Chapter 3).

The *Laboratorio* is administratively part of CORFO, the Chilean Economic Development Agency (under the auspices of the Ministry of Economy), and has a governing board composed of five ministries (including the Ministry of the Economy, the General Secretariat of the Presidency, the Ministry of Finance, the Ministry of Social Development, and the Ministry of Interior and Public Security), CORFO, the National Civil Service Directorate, and three members of civil society.

In carrying out its programme and activities, the *Laboratorio* uses a wide range of innovative methods from human-centred design to prototyping, from the use of experiments to co-creation, from engaging individual institutions to calls for open innovation. Through their skills and capabilities building a stream of activity, the *Laboratorio* is engaging with employees of public institutions to teach innovative methods and build their capabilities to innovate.

The *Laboratorio* has set up partnerships with different public institutions through evolving programmes that give public employees the chance to use and learn about innovative tools, mainly through developing and implementing their own innovation projects. In terms of recent initiatives, the participation of public institutions and their civil servants has largely been via public calls for proposals and interest from public institutions followed by a selection procedure (Box 2.4, the *Experimenta* programme, the latter bringing 12 institutions into the first version of the programme).

The wider institutional context supporting innovation

OECD research (2017) has pointed to the central nature of the role of the state in encouraging public sector innovation by setting the conditions and lowering the barriers for innovation. Yet there is relatively little evidence of how countries are organising and co-ordinating their innovation portfolio and initiatives across central government entities.

Emerging models include more decentralised approaches – such as in Australia, where various agencies are in advance on different aspects of a loose innovation agenda. Support is provided by a senior leader's Innovation Champions Group acting as a forum for sharing lessons and co-ordinating inter-agency collaboration; to more centralised ones. In Denmark, consolidation of a key innovation portfolio (digital, management, innovation) under a dedicated Public Sector Innovation Minister. Canada has implemented a more hybrid model where a federal high-level co-ordination platform for innovation initiatives (Minister's Innovation Committee) allows for the discussion of joint priorities and enables experiences to be shared and joint learning.

The institutional framework supporting innovation in Chile is fragmented and includes a wide constellation of actors with formal but loosely co-ordinated mandates to support innovation. These include:

- **The Innovation Division of the Ministry of the Economy**: This division plays a role in co-ordinating and contributing to the wider institutional framework for public sector innovation. It is in charge of establishing the guidelines for the 2014-2018 National Innovation Policy, which includes public sector innovation in the framework of innovation for inclusive growth, and is currently leading the drafting of a policy for public sector innovation. It chairs the board of the *Laboratorio*.
- **The General Secretariat of the Presidency (SEGPRES), Modernisation and Digital Government unit**: the State Modernisation and Digital Government Unit (*Unidad de Modernización del Estado y Gobierno Electrónico*) is responsible for initiatives relevant to spur ICT use for the purpose of improving relations between the state and its citizens and improving efficiency. Additionally, SEGPRES is responsible for the co-ordination and follow up of the implementation of all current and future initiatives affecting the development of digital government. SEGPRES is represented on the *Laboratorio* Board.
- **The Modernisation Unit in the Ministry of Finance**: This Unit is responsible for the modernisation of government and its services. In 2012 and 2013, it developed the "*Desafío Chile Gestiona*" contest aimed at recognising and rewarding initiatives that improve the management and the benefits that public services deliver to citizens. From 2014, the National Directorate of Civil Service created the *Funciona!* Award, aimed at rewarding teams of civil servants that have implemented innovations within their institutions. This Ministry and the Unit are represented on the *Laboratorio* Board.
- **CORFO, the Chilean Economic Development Agency**: hosts the *Laboratorio* and, while mainly involved in promoting innovation in the private sector, also has some objectives related to public sector innovation. Its mission is to "improve the competitiveness and diversification of the country by encouraging investment, innovation and entrepreneurship" and also has representation on the *Laboratorio* Board.
- **National Council for Innovation and Development (CNID)**: the CNID advises the President on the identification, formulation and implementation of policies to strengthen innovation, competitiveness and development in Chile and proposes public as well as private action. One of the priorities for the CNID is to encourage innovation in the public sector. The *Laboratorio* is working with the CNID on a project to start making case studies of Chilean public sector innovation systematic.
- **The National Civil Service Directorate (DNSC)**: has among its objectives "being leader in matters of employment and quality of working life, implementing policies and innovative practices for the public sector". The DNSC plays a key role in setting guidelines and recommendations for the development and recruitment of the civil service, including the Senior Civil Service (ADP, *Alta Dirección Pública*). It currently co-ordinates the *Funciona!* Innovation award

(previously called *Desafío Innovación*), which recognises the ability of analysis, creativity, innovation and improvement in the management of implemented processes by civil servants.

HRM and public sector innovation in Chile

Recognising the important lever HRM can be for public sector innovation, the Chilean government is currently taking steps to further the innovation mandate by seeking to understand how its HR functions and structures can be used to build civil servants' capabilities to innovate. The following section summarises the key characteristics of the HRM system in Chile to provide a baseline on which to assess how HR functions can improve the workforces' capabilities to innovate.

The HR system in Chile is fairly decentralised, meaning that many HR functions are performed at organisational level. While this can present challenges related to the harmonisation of HR processes and methods across the central public administration, it is not uncommon in OECD countries (Figure 1.3).

Figure 1.3. Extent of delegation of HRM practices to line ministries in central government in OECD countries (2016)

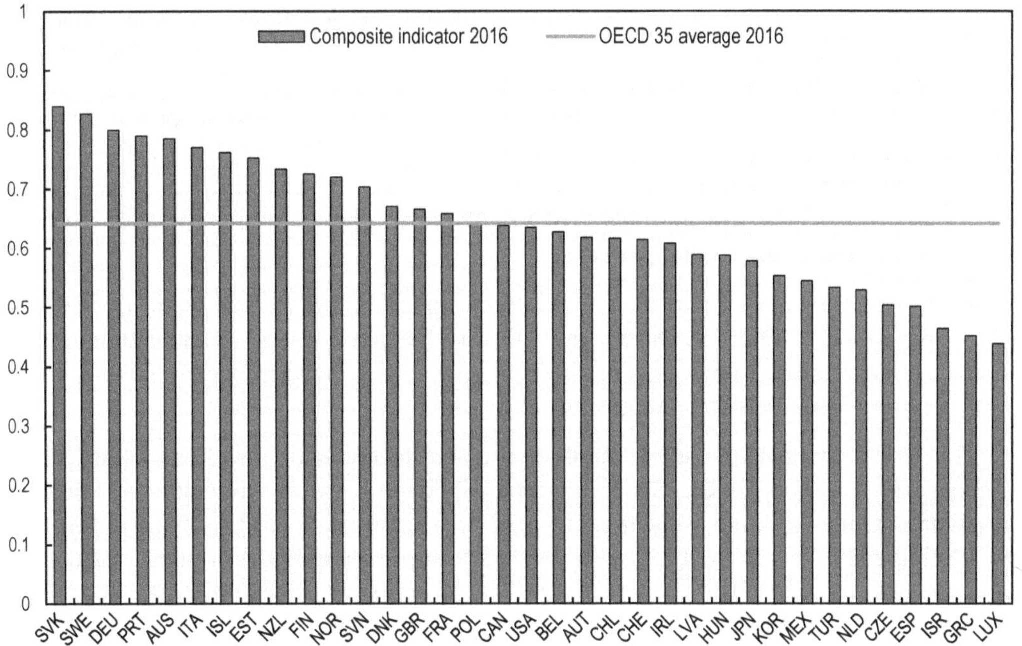

Note: This index summarises the relative level of authority provided to line ministries to make HRM decisions. It does not evaluate how well line ministries are using this authority. It is composed of the following variables: the existence of a central HRM body, and the role of line Ministries in determining; the number and types of posts within organisations; the allocation of the budget between payroll and other expenses; staff compensation levels; position classification, recruitment and dismissals; and conditions of employment. The index ranges from 0 (no delegation) to 1 (high level of delegation). Missing data for countries were estimated by mean replacement. The variables composing the index and their relative importance are based on expert judgements. Additional information: www.oecd.org/gov/pem/OECD%20HRM%20Country%20Profiles%20-%20Methodological%20Notes.pdf.

Source: OECD 2016 Survey on Strategic Human Resources Management in Central/Federal Governments of OECD Countries.

With the exception of the management of senior leaders, Chile's central HR authority's role has been limited to providing recommendations or guidelines on how such functions should be conducted. Example of this can be seen in the organisation of many HR functions including the following:

- **Recruitment**: There are different categories of public employees, those of civil servants that are permanent (*planta*) and those that have contracts with specific elements of the public administration (*contrata*). Although many may perform similar functions, they are recruited through different processes. Except for senior managers, the recruitment into the civil service (for *planta* and *contrata*) is conducted by each public organisation, depending on its needs, with little standardisation. The DNSC therefore only plays a role in setting guidelines and recommended standards for the recruitment process. For example, the DNSC's Manual for Selection Procedures provides recommendations that aim at providing support to institutions in the processes for recruiting civil servants. There is no common competency framework for middle managers and, as such, the recruitment of middle managers is very similar to the above-mentioned recruitment of public employees.
- **Training and Mobility**: Similarly to the recruitment system, the development of the competencies of public employees is also determined at organisation level. Each organisation within the central public administration is responsible for identifying current and future training needs and producing an organisational learning plan, including an initial training programme for civil servants. The role of the DNSC is to provide guidance to public institutions and support them in the preparation of an analysis of training needs, planning, implementation and an evaluation of the effect of the institution's Annual Training Plan. There are no current specific programmes for mobility in the public administration; however DNSC has noted plans to increase it.
- **Performance**: In Chile, the DNSC draws up guidelines to help institutions design performance criteria. Once again, this is managed on an organisational level. However, the SADP or senior civil servant cadre is managed by the DNSC, with a common competency framework.

The DNSC manages most HR functions related to the senior leaders of the Chilean public sector (as part of the SADP system), including the recruitment and selection procedures. Chilean Senior Management generally corresponds to the two top layers of the administrative hierarchy: the positions of Director General and Deputies, in agencies, and heads of division. With the exception of a minority of politically appointed Senior Managers, most positions are part of the *Sistema de Alta Dirección Pública* (SADP). The SADP works as a filter, selecting the most suitable candidates for specific senior public executive positions, but leaving the final decision to the political authority.

A new law (No. 20.955) approved in October 2016 introduces important changes in the area of HR management and in the SADP system. In the area of HR management for example, the law established a Sub-Directorate in charge of Management and Staff Development (*Subdireccion de gestion y desarollo de personas*) within the DNSC. This may support the DNSC in having a more controlling role with regards to integrity, recruitment, selection, development and retention of civil servants, as well as in good labour practices.

This means that while DNSC's current role is mainly about providing guidance to other government institutions, it is possible that with the new Law the DNSC will play a stronger role in setting common standards, oversight and take a more proactive stance in HR areas.

Similarly, this new Law also increases the scope of action of the DNSC with regards to the Senior Civil Service. In an effort to improve the efficiency of the SADP, it increases the number of senior positions for which recruitment needs to be made through the system. It also has provisions to improve the performance management of SADP staff, to reduce the impact of government changes on senior positions in the administration, and to improve the processes for selection and recruitment for ADP positions.

Currently, a typical selection process in the SADP takes around three months, beginning with the publication of the vacancy in the media. A consultancy, commissioned by the Council, analyses the curricula of the different candidates and prepares a shortlist for selection by the Council or a selection committee. The Council for Senior Executive Service (*Consejo de Alta Dirección Pública*) is responsible for guaranteeing the transparency, confidentiality and non-discrimination of the selection process. The council is chaired by the director of the DNSC and is formed by four members proposed by the President of the Republic and approved by the Senate.

With the HR system in the Chilean public sector largely decentralised, and considering the transition period towards the full implementation of the new law, it will be important to consider how public institutions can best make use of HRM practices that can improve the innovation capacity of public employees, and how to communicate and convince HR authorities in public sector organisations of the value in adopting such practices. As the DNSC begins to take on a greater role in developing common standards, there is also an opportunity to bring the links between HRM and public sector innovation into consideration and to make an impact across the central public administration.

The three chapters that follow take a closer look into the abilities (Chapter 2), motivations (Chapter 3), and opportunities (Chapter 4) required for the Chilean civil service to innovate – and propose concrete recommendations (Chapter 5) for the *Laboratorio* and other organisations of the Chilean government to strengthen the innovation capacities of their civil service.

Notes

1 According to the 2016 Survey on Strategic Human Resources Management in Central/Federal Governments of OECD Countries.

2 From President Bachelet's Presidential Address, May 21, 2014: http://derechoyreligion.uc.cl/es/docman/documentacion/chile/otros/519-discurso-presidencial-y-cuenta-publica-21-de-mayo-de-2014-discurso/file.

References

Borins, Sandford (2014), *The Persistence of Innovation in Government*, Brookings Institution Press, Washington, DC.

Boxall, Peter and John Purcell (2011), *Strategy and Human Resource Management*, Third Edition, Palgrave Mcmillan.

Hartley, Jean (2006), "Innovation in Governance and Public Services: Past and Present", *Public Money & Management*, 25:1, 27-34.

OECD (2017), *Fostering Innovation in the Public Sector*, OECD Publishing, Paris. http://dx.doi.org/10.1787/9789264270879-en.

OECD (2016), *Engaging Public Employees for a High-Performing Civil Service*, OECD Public Governance Reviews, OECD Publishing, Paris, http://dx.doi.org/10.1787/9789264267190-en.

OECD (2015), *The Innovation Imperative in the Public Sector: Setting an Agenda for Action*, OECD Publishing, Paris, http://dx.doi.org/10.1787/9789264236561-en.

OECD (2013), *Government at a Glance 2013*, OECD Publishing, Paris, http://dx.doi.org/10.1787/gov_glance-2013-en.

Annex 1.A

The innovation imperative: A call for action

The OECD has charted the factors that turn out to have played a role in creating innovative capacity of governments. These include the management of human resources, the flow of knowledge within and across organisations, the organisation of work, and the rules and processes that govern operations and activities. Governments are called on to take the following action to strengthen these areas so as to boost their innovative capacities.

ACTION 1: Focus on people

Governments must invest in the capacity and capabilities of civil servants as the catalysts of innovation. This includes building the culture, incentives and norms to facilitate new ways of working.

No government can build a strong and secure country without a professional, capable and innovative civil service. As demands on the public sector and corresponding resources continue to move in opposing directions, an innovative public service will be increasingly vital to ensuring both domestic and global success. Given the far-reaching impact of the public sector, all governments have a stake in ensuring that their public services are equipped with the skills, incentives and scope for smart risk taking and problem solving to spur innovation and drive better outcomes for citizens.

ACTION 2: Put knowledge to use

Governments must facilitate the free flow of information, data and knowledge across the public sector and use it to respond creatively to new challenges and opportunities.

The information, data and knowledge that inform strategic and operational decision making are critical to fuelling public sector innovation. Harnessing the innovative potential of information requires that information be open and available, and that organisations carefully consider what information is required and how best to systematically integrate it into the decision making process to support continuous learning. Organisations who fail to learn risk incurring higher costs and repeating their errors, while failing to realise new possibilities.

ACTION 3: Working together

Governments must advance new organisational structures and leverage partnerships to enhance approaches and tools, share risk and harness available information and resources for innovation.

The complex problems faced by governments today require new ways of working. These include approaches based on collaboration and partnership which integrate the vital perspectives of citizens, civil society, academia and business, as well as exchange within the public sector. Creating more open, networked, and horizontal organisations, adept at collaboration inside and outside government are required. So too are more flexible approaches to working, including pooling talent and creating multidisciplinary management teams to strengthen collaboration. Temporary teams, pilot projects and short-term assignments are all ways for governments to experiment and better align talent and resources to encourage dialogue, experimentation, risk-taking, problem-solving and innovation.

ACTION 4: Rethink the rules

Government must ensure that internal rules and processes are balanced in their capacity to mitigate risks while protecting resources and enabling innovation.

While internal controls, rules and processes are required to ensure sound stewardship and accountability, they can inadvertently stifle innovation. To guard against this, governments must ensure that their public services are marked by reasonable rules and lean processes. Such efforts should ensure that the accountability regime is both robust and easy to navigate while also more systematically focused on enabling innovation, and working horizontally to achieve shared objectives. New outcome-focused approaches to project management are one step in moving away from the rigidities of a command-and-control model.

Reference

OECD (2015), *The Innovation Imperative in the Public Sector: Setting an Agenda for Action*, OECD Publishing, Paris, http://dx.doi.org/10.1787/9789264236561-en.

Chapter 2.

Abilities for public sector innovation in Chile

This chapter discusses the innovation-oriented abilities, skills and competencies of Chile's public employees and recommends ways that these can be improved through recruitment and development. The definition of innovation skills in the public sector is evolving, and the OECD has developed a framework that identifies six key skills areas: iteration, data literacy, citizen centricity, curiosity, storytelling and insurgency. The assessment suggests that Chile may benefit from development of abilities related to iterative project management and co-creation with citizens. The chapter also underlines that challenges and opportunities for aligning recruitment and development programmes with innovation skills. It underlines the potential of developing and managing cross-organisational mobility programmes as one way of developing and spreading innovation skills across the public sector.

Which skills for public sector innovation?

People are central to public sector innovation at every stage of its process. As such, the study of innovation must begin with an understanding of the people who contribute to innovation, and what motivates them and enables them to do so (OECD, 2015).

The abilities and skills of public employees are essential elements in public sector innovation. An analysis by the Australian Department of Industry[1] in the framework of the APS 200 project on public sector innovation identifies the lack of skills as a "major barrier to generate, select, implement and sustain public sector innovation".

Recognising that public employees are at the centre of public sector innovation first of all raises questions about which skills public employees need to innovate (OECD, 2015). Innovation is not a skill or ability in itself, but the combination of a variety of elements that come together in the right place and time. In this regard, understanding the skills and attributes people require in order to contribute to innovation is an important step in the policy-making process.

So far there has been very little work done on innovation skills, particularly in a public sector context. In general, individual abilities can be thought of in terms of technical skills, (defined and testable knowledge and technical abilities such as the ability to use certain tools) and "softer" competencies (behaviours, orientations, but also the ability to make connections between ideas that are not apparent, to ask the right questions and network with the right people, etc.). OECD (2011) work on innovation skills in the private sector identifies three types of abilities required for innovation:

- Subject Specific – the technical skills and knowledge associated with the subject area being innovated. This would be, for example, computer programming skills for developing software innovations, or medical knowledge to innovate in the health sector. In a public sector context this might include policy analysis skills in a specific policy field (e.g. tax policy, housing policy, or educational policy), financial analysis, big data analytics, etc.
- Thinking and Creativity – the ability to ask the right questions, to identify the gaps and develop creative solutions and approaches that can help fill these gaps. This includes the ability to look across seemingly disparate data, cases, problems and processes to identify common threads and connect the dots. Imagination and curiosity are drivers. These are more difficult to assess using traditional selection and assessment methods, and are not developed easily in traditional classroom-based learning environments.
- Behavioural and Social – recognising that innovation is a team sport places a high level of significance on the team's ability to work in partnerships, communicate, negotiate, network and collaborate. Leadership is required to draw out the right skills in the team and a level of confidence is needed to take the kinds of risks that result in learning and growth.

Dyer, Gregersen and Christensen (2011) identify five transversal skills which contribute to innovation. The most fundamental, "associative thinking", describes how one synthesises new information and makes connections across concepts. "Put simply, innovative thinkers connect fields, problems, or ideas that others find unrelated". The rest of the skills support associative thinking. They are: questioning (even more than answering), observing (implies being close to those you serve and the world around the service), networking (to find and test ideas among people with "radically" different views), experimenting (holding convictions at bay and testing hypotheses).

Innovation in the public sector is different from the private sector and therefore likely to require a different skill set. For example, the challenges facing the public sector are particularly complex and the bottom line not always clear. Public sector contexts tend to be rules-based and highly regulated, political and contested. Funding for innovation is harder to identify and has higher standards related to transparency and accountability. Taking in combination, this leads to higher levels of risk aversion and slower rates of change and adoption. The multitude of differences between public and private sector operating environments suggest that skills for public sector innovators, while sometimes similar, will differ in a number of important ways, and therefor require their own consideration.

Employment systems in the public sector also tend to be less responsive to changing circumstances, making it harder to get specific skill sets in place to address innovation challenges. This last point is important as the skills and abilities required to achieve public sector innovation well are highly varied depending on the innovation context and therefore demand employment systems that can attract, select and retain a wide variety of skill sets. For example, the needed skill set is likely to be influenced by the stage of innovation (e.g. the initial phase of an innovation may require skills related to observation and communication with users, while the development phase may require iteration and experimentation skills), by the type of innovation (e.g. the innovation of a product may require engineering skills, whereas innovation in a service may require change management skills), and by the service area where innovation takes place (innovate in a highly regulated sector like public procurement may require substantial legal skills).

As a result, it is likely that institutions will differ in terms of their skills needs at a given time. In such a changing context, recruiting and training people with different backgrounds, experience or mindsets may be helpful to be able to draw on such diversity when developing innovations, as suggested by Australia's Department of Industry.[2]

The OECD is currently working with various partners to better understand innovation skills in a public sector context and the complementarity of skills at team level. This exploratory research is based on in-depth interviews with civil servants around the world (including Chile) who have been involved in innovation projects, activities and teams, as well as public sector innovation specialists.

Figure 2.1. Emerging innovation skills model – six skills categories

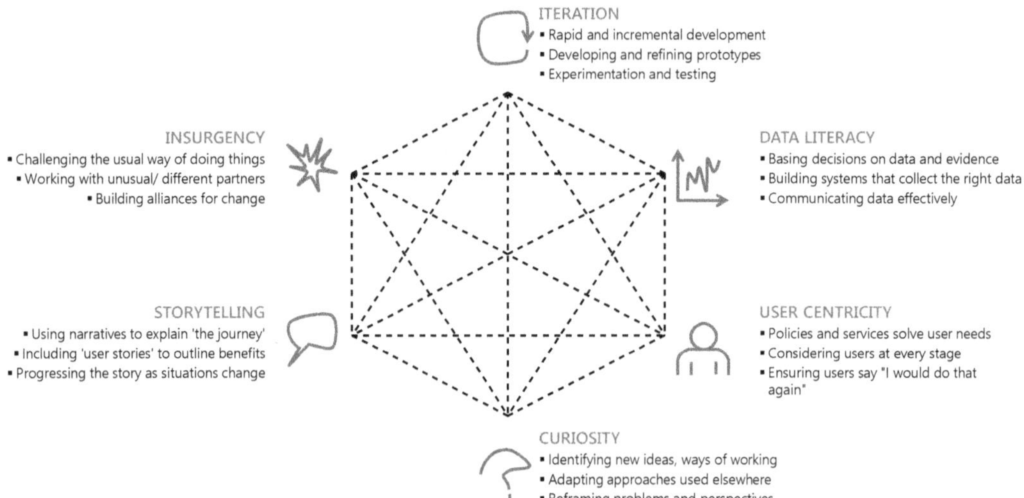

The findings emerging from the research identify some common themes in the skills and capabilities of innovators which the OECD team has grouped under the following six categories (Figure 2.1):

- Iteration: skills to incrementally and experimentally develop public policies and services. These suggest skills related to prototyping and experimental policy design, and to bring policy, implementation and evaluation skills together under a more agile approach to project management.
- Data literacy: skills to leverage data to inform innovation projects at every stage of their lifecycle. This implies skills to analyse and link existing data sets to bring new insights, collect new data, and to translate the data insights into actionable innovation.
- User centricity: skills that bring public employees closer to the citizens they serve to ensure that services are focused on responding to user needs. Skills that may be used here can include ethnographic observation, outreach and communication, facilitation and networking skills with user groups and stakeholders.
- Curiosity: skills that start with asking questions, seeking out and trying new ideas or ways of working. It requires skills to actively scan beyond one's own day-to-day work to identify surprising developments and to connect the dots to bring insights one's own work.
- Storytelling: skills that can explain desired change in a way that builds support and engages the right people at the right level. This may mean suggesting ideas to funders, decision makers, allies and partners, and, ultimately the public at large.
- Insurgency: skills that enable innovators to challenge the status quo and working with unusual partners to implement change. This requires building coalitions within and outside government, and an intimate knowledge of decision-making processes and how to influence them.

The next phase of this work will further unfold these themes and look at who should possess these skills and to what degree. This suggests the need to look at them in two ways: some awareness of them for most public servants (e.g. what does this mean and how could it be applied to my area of work?) combined with practitioner-level skills for those directly using these skills in their day-to-day work. As a first look at these specialist skills, the research will look at "design-led" and "data-led" innovators (Box 2.1) to provide a tangible way of discerning some of the specific differences in their skill sets compared to mainstream civil servants. These differences will have different implications for HR development: building the innovation skills at an awareness level in the general workforce will require a different strategy comparted to specialist skills.

Box 2.1. Design and Data-led specialist skills for public sector innovation

"Design-led innovators" use a mix of design-thinking and participatory research skills; in particular they take a user-centred approach to identifying solutions to policy problems, for example:

- by using ethnographic methods and action research approaches to work closely with service users and gain a deep understanding of their needs
- by understanding how people interact with systems and interfaces they design services where it is easy for users to understand what they need to do and easy for them to do it
- borrowing from industrial and product design practices they develop solutions by testing prototypes that are repeatedly 'tweaked' through an iterative process with users rather than only testing a near-final solution with them
- by using visual and communication design skills they are able to convey messages and complex ideas in more engaging ways.

"Data-led innovators" use a mix of traditional analytical approaches with newer data science techniques so that decisions are based on data rather than opinions, for example:

- by using large/unstructured data and/or from multiple sources ("big data") they can analyse subsets of user populations and identify trends that may not be detected in sample surveys
- by using real-time data feeds and alert service managers on issues and problems as they emerge rather than after they have arisen
- by using machine learning techniques, they can identify relationships and find models that would not be found with traditional statistical/econometric techniques, including through analysis of large text-based data sets
- by using new data visualisation techniques, including interactive methods, to communicate results they can help people to engage with insights from the data.

Source: OECD (forthcoming), Core skills for public sector innovation: a model of skills to promote and enable innovation in public sector organisations.

Assessment of abilities for innovation in Chile

When asked to reflect on the skills used to implement innovative projects, Chilean public employees mention a wide range of skills in line with those described in the literature and the skills models presented above. For example, in interviews and workshops, many discussed the importance of empathising with users, testing ideas through iteration, communicating effectively with decision makers, anticipating various scenarios, and managing complex projects, risks, and multidisciplinary teams (Box 2.2).

Box 2.2. Innovation skills and competencies highlighted by Chilean civil servants

The OECD conducted a first data collection process during a week-long review mission to Santiago in November 2015 during which the OECD team, including two peer reviewers from France and the United States, undertook various interviews, focus groups and round tables with over 90 key stakeholders from the *Laboratorio* and its governing board officials, from other ministries, municipalities, civil society organisations, trade unions, innovators, the private sector and academics. While these stakeholders were very diverse, they all agreed that innovation in Chile's public sector is necessary to drive progress and displayed an enthusiasm and commitment to making it a reality.

The workshops allowed investigating the different types of skills and abilities that innovators and their managers use to innovate and manage innovation in the public sector. The following abilities were identified:

- listen to, and empathize with service users and other stakeholders, in order to discover the challenges they face when approaching and using the service
- knowledge of the mission and context of the public institution, in order to design solutions that make sense in that context
- ability to test an idea on a small scale, which requires the ability to anticipate, to test different hypotheses, to project different scenarios, and to have the capacity to react quickly and to adapt to results
- capacity to work in/manage multi-disciplinary teams in order to understand various approaches to a given situation and to be able to address it from different perspectives
- resilience and perseverance, and the capacity to react to a changing context, for example regarding political support or user satisfaction
- convince others to get their buy-in
- have good project management skills, which involve the ability to manage deadlines, risks, people and outcomes, but also expectations from users, from the administrative hierarchy and even from the political level
- evaluate the impact of an innovation including a good knowledge of the process but also of appropriate impact assessment methodologies, data and resources.

Source: OECD Workshops in Chile.

While the OECD found some examples of all six skill areas in use among Chile's public employees, the general perception that emerged from interviews, workshops and desk research is that these skills exist in pockets with little framework to bring them together and mainstream them throughout the administration. The team had the impression that public sector innovation in Chile is primarily top-down, and that Chilean civil servants lack the skills and opportunities to persuade end-users of services to participate in production.

Chilean civil servants involved in innovative projects spent a great deal of time discussing their use of the aspects of the last three skill areas. Curiosity was displayed by their participation in networks, although they expressed a desire for more opportunities to build this skill set, and more time in their day-to-day work to explore possible solutions for their policy problems. Storytelling was often emphasised as necessary to build support for their innovation. Insurgency was evoked when many innovators discussed the importance of knowing the administration and how to change it from the inside. Conversely, the review team did not find as much evidence of iterative processes, or data-driven innovation.

A particular gap was noticed in the citizen-centred skills area. While many innovators emphasised the need to empathise with service users, few showed evidence of putting that into practice. It seems that many of the innovations discussed in the context of the missions and workshops were focused internally – on generating ideas from staff. Moving from staff to service users is a leap that requires a certain level of confidence that may not yet exist in many of Chile's public services. This was an opinion echoed by many of the key stakeholders interviewed for this report. This may be an area that would be worth investing in training, which is currently being tested with the *Experimenta programme* run by the *Laboratorio* (Box 2.4).

Many of the public employees who participated in the study expressed a lack of training for skills development broadly, and for innovation-oriented skills more specifically. On multiple occasions, it was suggested that most training is focused on information updates related to, for example, a change in regulation. What innovation-oriented training does exist was seen as being too short and time bound to make a difference in business-as-usual. Innovators expressed a desire to learn how to experiment and back up their ideas with sound research, to build their case and structure their projects. Most successful innovators spoke of having to learn it all along the way.

Some of these insights are reflected in a pilot exercise that was conducted with a group of 20 public sector innovators from 15 different public institutions and services (Box 2.3). Given the small sample size, these results cannot be generalised, however they present some initial indications of how this group of Chilean public innovators perceive their innovation-oriented abilities, those of their management and their organisation's readiness to incorporate these skills.

Not surprisingly, this group sees their own abilities as surpassing their managers and their organisations' readiness in every skill area. However, data literacy is a particular area where innovators perceive a greater degree of organisational readiness. This may reflect a general perception that was often articulated during fact-finding missions, that public sector innovation in Chile is generally associated with technology rather than with people. The areas of iteration and user-centred skills score the lowest on the innovator's self-assessment, with most innovators stating that they have a general awareness of these skills areas but do not use them regularly.

Each of these six skills areas are broken into subcomponents in the survey. The three subcomponents in which innovators' self-assessments were noticeably low were: using incremental/iterative project management approaches (e.g. Agile); using experiments to evaluate pilots, projects and policies; and using behavioural science techniques (e.g. "nudge") in public policy. Additional research could be done to confirm these skills gaps and could help to inform the design of training programmes.

Box 2.3. Innovation skills perception survey: Pilot

During the final workshop of the project, a pilot survey was completed by civil servants that acts as a tool to assess one's own innovation-oriented skills, and perception of management capacity and organisational readiness to use innovation skills. The survey is structured on the six skills areas identified by the OECD: iteration, data literacy, user-centered, curiosity, storytelling, and insurgency. Each of these skills areas are further subdivided until subcomponents and participants are asked to rate each subcomponent on a simple three-point scale against three dimensions: their own awareness/proficiency of the skill, encouragement from their manager to use the skill, and their organisation's readiness to adopt the skill.

Figure 2.2. Pilot skills survey outcomes

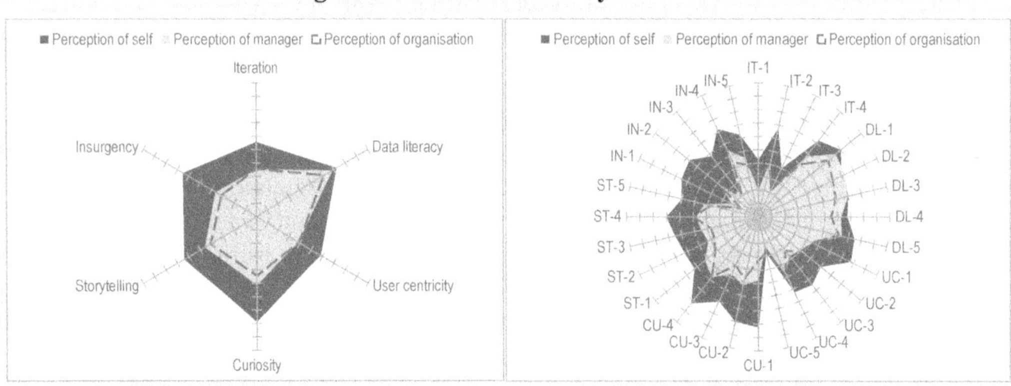

The results of this pilot survey are shown above. In all skills areas, the 20 innovator's self-perception is higher than their perception of their managers' support or their organisation's readiness. While the sample size is far too small to generalise, the noticeable impression from this survey is that public innovators perceive data literacy as a skill area that is far more supported than the rest. Furthermore, innovators see particular skills gaps in areas related to iteration and user-centred skills, particularly in the use of behavioural insights.

This kind of perception study could provide valuable insights into future studies. For example, the tool could be used within an agency in various/all units to get an understanding of employee perceptions and how they vary. It could also be used to compare organisations and benchmark them against each other. This can help to provide information on training, recruitment and organisational development, and provide input into management decision making. It can also help to identify areas with higher concentration of innovation and managerial skills and good practices that can be shared within and across organisations.

The subcomponents of the six skills areas are shown in the chart on the right. They are:

S1	Iteration	S4	Curiosity
IT-1	Using incremental/iterative project management approaches (e.g. Agile)	CU-1	Asking questions or analysing a situation from different perspectives
IT-2	Using prototypes to develop and explore how different approaches work	CU-2	Seeking out feedback about how a service can be improved
IT-3	Using experiments to evaluate pilots, projects and policies	CU-3	Identifying approaches that work elsewhere and adapting them for your own project/team/service
IT-4	Risk taking and management	CU-4	Working in teams with diverse perspectives and backgrounds

Box 2.3. Innovation skills perception survey: Pilot *(continued)*

S2	**Data literacy**	**S5**	**Storytelling**
DL-1	Collecting useful, relevant and timely data	ST-1	Explaining how a project delivers positive changes
DL-2	Accessing existing data collected by the government	ST-2	Using multiple methods to communicate project information (e.g. video, infographics, blog posts, etc.)
DL-3	Working effectively with analysts and data specialists	ST-3	Using "user stories" to explain problems or changes from the user's perspective
DL-4	Communicating data analysis and results to non-specialists	ST-4	Adapting the message as the situation develops or audience changes
DL-5	Basing decisions on data and evidence	ST-5	Communicating the results of the project after it is finished to promote learning and diffusion
S3	**User centricity**	**S6**	**Insurgency**
UC-1	Considering the users of public services at every stage of a project	IN-1	Trying out untested or unusual ways of working, even if they may not work
UC-2	Conducting research to find out what users really need from public services	IN-2	Working with new and different partners to deliver projects
UC-3	Facilitating interactive workshops with users to develop or test approaches	IN-3	Challenging traditional or default positions and perspectives
UC-4	Developing partnerships with organisations that represent users	IN-4	Understanding how the organisation works and how to change it
UC-5	Using behavioural science techniques (e.g. "nudge) in public policy	IN-5	Building coalitions to drive change and amplify messages

Source: OECD workshops in Chile.

Acquiring and reinforcing these skills from an organisational perspective requires thinking about two fundamental HR functions to ensure that the right people with the right skills and talents are working in the right ways to maximise creative energy and see projects through to implementation: recruitment to bring people in, and development to build the skills of the existing workforce. This means opening positions to external (or internal) sources of recruitment; selecting people based on the right combinations of technical skills and behavioural competencies, and values. Second, innovation skills can be developed with a team and long-term orientation and the participation of employees in the design of training activities can help build innovation capacity. Recruitment and training of civil servants and managers will be the focus of the next sections.

Recruiting public sector innovators: trends and challenges in the Chilean context

Recruitment and selection systems bring people with desired skill sets into organisations and teams to accomplish tasks and deliver on government priorities. Chile is among 20 OECD countries which aspire to a more innovative civil service in their strategic vision documents (Figure 2.3). Given this priority, recruitment and selection systems should be designed to get the right people with the right skill sets into the right positions to contribute to innovation. Out of the 20 OECD countries which include innovation in their civil service visions, 12 report using recruitment procedures to build the innovative capacity of the workforce.

The link between public sector recruitment and innovation is recognised in the USA, where the Strategy for American Innovation aims at delivering innovative government in part by "rapidly hiring top talent using flexible hiring authorities and accelerated hiring practices, particularly for areas where there is a significant gap between world-class performance and current public-sector practices".[3] In addition, to increase inclusiveness and diversity in the civil service, countries like Canada are encouraging innovation in recruitment and staffing procedures by simplifying the job application process or introducing internship programmes.

Figure 2.3. Elements highlighted in strategic civil service visions in OECD countries

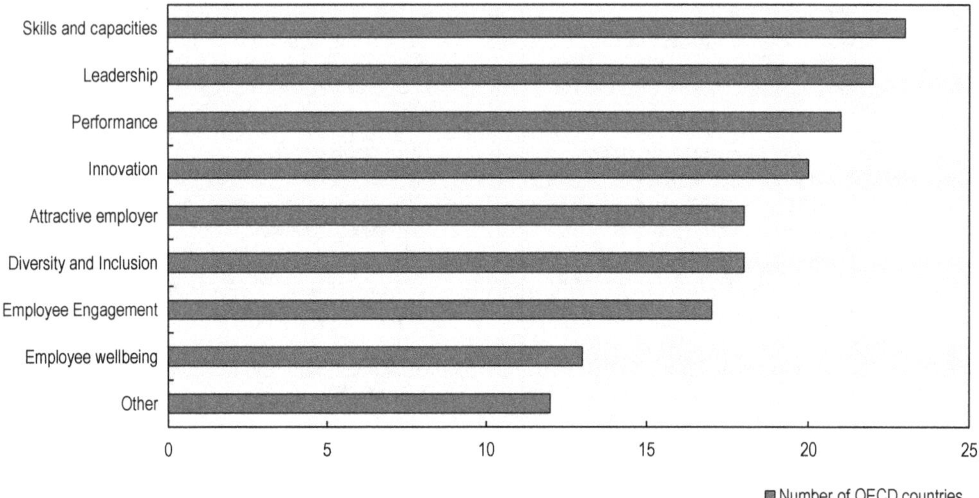

Source: 2016 Survey on Strategic Human Resource Management in Central/Federal Governments of OECD Countries.

The challenge in Chile

Within the current regulatory framework in Chile the recruitment of public employees (with the exception of senior managers) is a process conducted by each organisation with a high degree of autonomy and little standardisation. No central authority exists to design and implement reforms that could align recruitment practices to innovation skills, but as the DNSC is expected to assume a standard-setting role with the Law 20.955/2016, the DNSC could give priority to innovation in these areas while continuing to seek to influence through guidance and support.

This is further complicated as the recruitment process differs according to the category of public employees. The two main categories of public employees are civil servants whose work conditions are regulated by the *Estatuto Administrativo* (*planta*), and other employees who have specific contracts with public administrations (*contrata*). While middle managers can be either of these categories, the recruitment of senior managers is subject to different rules and will be discussed later in this chapter.

Currently, many institutions are aware and involved in innovation initiatives in the public sector; however, in these institutions there was no indication that innovation-oriented skill-sets are identified and actively recruited (except for the employees of the *Laboratorio*). This is likely for a number of reasons. First, as discussed above, there is little agreement on what constitutes innovation skills in public sector contexts, and how these translate from one sector to another. The six innovation skills areas proposed by the OECD project begin to address this issue. Second, most public sector recruitment practices are oriented towards ensure equal merit-based opportunities, and thus objectively give priority to defined skills mainly identified through certified (e.g. university) education. The kinds of softer behavioural competencies that are required of innovators, such as curiosity, storytelling, or even insurgency, are harder to identify and assess. Third, most public employment systems have a tendency towards recruiting policy generalists (e.g. people with degrees in economics, law, political science, public administration, etc.) and are often not well designed to attract and select people with more specialist skill sets such as designers, data scientists and facilitation experts.

Opportunities for the DNSC to support more innovation-oriented recruitment and selection

The DNSC already has some tools that could be adjusted to help support innovation-oriented recruitment at institutional level. The Manual for Selection procedures aims at supporting institutions in the recruitment processes of civil servants, and also encourages them to adopt an innovative approach regarding their policies and practices of people management. In this regard, the Manual already identifies some competencies for innovation as it encourages recruiters to assess candidates for innovative thinking, motivation to achieve, or strategic thinking.

In practice however, job profiles for civil servants include the skills and capabilities required to perform the function – these can be generic or more specific, but in each case they lead to the specific function that the institution is looking for. Skills related to innovation are usually not an explicit requirement in the job descriptions, suggesting that public institutions may not be very familiar with the concept of public sector innovation for better public services, or with the skills that can support it. In this sense, the DNSC has space to further explore the potential of the Manual to support innovation.

While the Manual dates back to 2006, the DNSC is currently working on a Plan for Advice on Recruitment and Selection (*Plan de Asesorías en Reclutamiento y Selección*) to reinforce merit-based recruitment through the development of policies, procedures and management tools. As the new Law 20.955/2016 also gives more responsibilities to the DNSC in the area of recruitment and selection of civil servants, this may provide an opportune window to include innovation-related skill sets and methods to assess these, in the tools that will support recruitment in the coming years.

In the preparation of the Plan for Advice on Recruitment and Selection, the DNSC could involve HR professionals or representatives from selection committees at institutional level (which are composed of the five highest positions of the institution's chief of staff) to discuss ways to include innovation skill sets and related competencies in the recruitment criteria.

In countries like France for example, the central HRM unit organises conferences to examine, with HR officials at Ministry and regional level, the implications of major guidelines on human resources management practices. These conferences, organised annually since 2007, combine technical meetings about management of the public workforce with strategic conferences about priorities in workforce planning.[4] This type of regular and short event involving HR professionals could be used by Chile to discuss innovation.

By involving HR and recruiting managers from a range of ministries, the DNSC could benefit from their field experience to develop a prototype innovation component for the *Plan*. A second phase of this process could involve inviting a number of institutions to test the prototype and adjust it in order to ensure maximal utility and relevance before launching it for broader use. Such an approach may not only benefit the end product, but could also raise awareness and get buy-in about the importance of recruiting for innovation from participating organisations.

Training people in selection committees to identify innovation-related skills during the recruitment process could also contribute to a more innovative civil service. This training could be built within the "*Decalogo*", a set of rules for selection committees developed by the DNSC to avoid selection bias and to promote better recruitment practices.

It is however important to note that while the foregoing recommendations regarding the Manual for Selection procedures, the Plan for Advice on Recruitment and Selection and the *Decalogo* cover the recruitment of civil servants, only 37% out of the 227 869 employees of the central public administration are civil servants (DIPRES, 2015).

Contrata positions: Balancing flexibility with merit.

For the remaining categories of public employees, namely *contrata* which are over 60% of the workforce, public services have the flexibility to recruit according to their needs. Having access to flexible recruitment procedures can support public sector innovation if it is used to attract specific skill sets to which general recruitment procedures are poorly adjusted. However in this case clear guidelines should exist for using such recruitment practices to avoid situations where two people with the same job have very different employment contracts. In Ireland, the Commission for Public Service Appointments has published a Code of Practice for Atypical Appointments which can be used in "appointment process where standard recruitment and selection approaches may not be appropriate to meet critical short-term needs and it is necessary to assign a specific serving civil servant or public servant to higher duties on a temporary basis for a defined short-term period to address such needs".[5]

In Chile, according to an institutional survey conducted by the DNSC in 2013 (*Barometro de la gestion de personas 2013*) transparent and merit-based selection criteria for c*ontrata* positions are used in less than half of the 171 respondent Central Public Administration institutions.[6] If one of the purposes of flexible hiring is to support public sector innovation, then administrations should make greater use of transparency and merit-based criteria for these positions, following the recommendation of the Presidential Instruction on Good Practices in Staff Development in the State (*Instructivo Presidencial sobre Buenas Prácticas Laborales en Desarrollo de Personas en el Estado*),[7] which encourages administrations to use comparable practices to recruit civil servants and *contrata* employees (including by making job profiles or descriptions for all positions regardless of its status). The new responsibilities given to the DNSC regarding staff recruitment and development (Law 20.955/2016) may improve DNSC's scope to act further in this direction.

Attractiveness of public employment: Employer branding for innovation

Finally, recruiting skills for public sector innovation also involves the capacity to attract those skills. This means ensuring that people with the skills and motivations to innovate in Chile's public sector are aware of employment opportunities where they can put these skills to use, and see the public sector as an attractive, trustworthy and credible employer. Chile's current employer branding promotes the concepts of integrity, public values, ethics, diversity, inclusion and opportunity to contribute to public value (OECD 2016 SHRM survey).

Adjusting this employer branding to attract public innovators could mean improving recruitment material to clearly identify innovation as a desired outcome and, therefore, mindset. Perhaps a starting point is the webpage where public employment positions are advertised,[8] used by all services of the Central Administration for the dissemination of job positions. Emphasising opportunities for public sector innovation, providing examples of innovative projects or even communicating about the public sector innovation activities and awards could attract candidates who are inspired to contribute to Public Sector Innovation (PSI).

It also suggests actively recruiting in places where potential public sector innovators are, such as employment fairs; innovation-oriented network events, conferences and awards ceremonies; graduate schools with innovation-oriented programming, and events in parallel with communication through social media. As the *Laboratorio* continues to expand its network of innovation professionals within and outside the public sector, it may be able to play a role in linking would-be innovators to jobs in the public institutions. This could be inspired by Bloomberg Philanthropies' innovation teams' programme[9] which brings innovation professionals to city government to "support agency leaders and staff through a data-driven process to assess problems, generate responsive new interventions, develop partnerships, and deliver measurable results".[10]

Of course care needs to be taken to ensure that communication matches reality and that applicants attracted by such communication strategies are placed in jobs that enable them to actively contribute their talents to public sector innovation. This could be accomplished through, for example, *Practicas Chile.*[11] This programme, managed by the DNSC and supported by the Ministry of Finance, offers university students the possibility to do an internship in Ministries and public services across the country. Emphasising innovation as part of the programme could be used to attract young talents, would give hosting institutions another opportunity to think about the innovative potential of job positions, and would also create a pool of potential future candidates to the civil service who would have acquired experience on public sector innovation.

In the United States for example, the InnovateGov Field Experience-Internship[12] in the State of Michigan gives an opportunity to university students to work with government agencies or non-profit organisations, namely in the City of Detroit, to address a complex set of issues surrounding the city's property foreclosures. The internships help students become involved in city or county politics, and include sessions with case discussion, peer consulting, and engagement or literature about urban innovation.

Developing skills for innovation

Learning is at the heart of public sector innovation. Innovating in the public sector is, by definition, a dynamic process of learning through observation, exchange, experimentation, testing, and debate. Each phase of an innovation project calls for different kinds of learning to inform the next. One team of Chilean public innovators expressed this idea in the context of one of the workshops when they told the group that to succeed they needed to, "learn how to learn".

Learning is increasingly seen in all knowledge-based professions as a fundamental part of the job. The initial learning received through pre-employment education is no longer considered sufficient to carry people through their entire career (OECD, 2011). As such, the concept of life-long learning is essential to ensure that the skills that individual employees have when recruited remain relevant for the workplace. In this sense, skills for innovation in the public sector cannot be static but will always be adjusting to new challenges, new operating environments, and new technological innovations and opportunities. For these reasons, looking at Chilean civil servants' capacities to learn, adapt and grow throughout their careers will be fundamental to building innovation capabilities in government.

Figure 2.4. Tools used for enabling innovation in the workforce in OECD countries (2016)

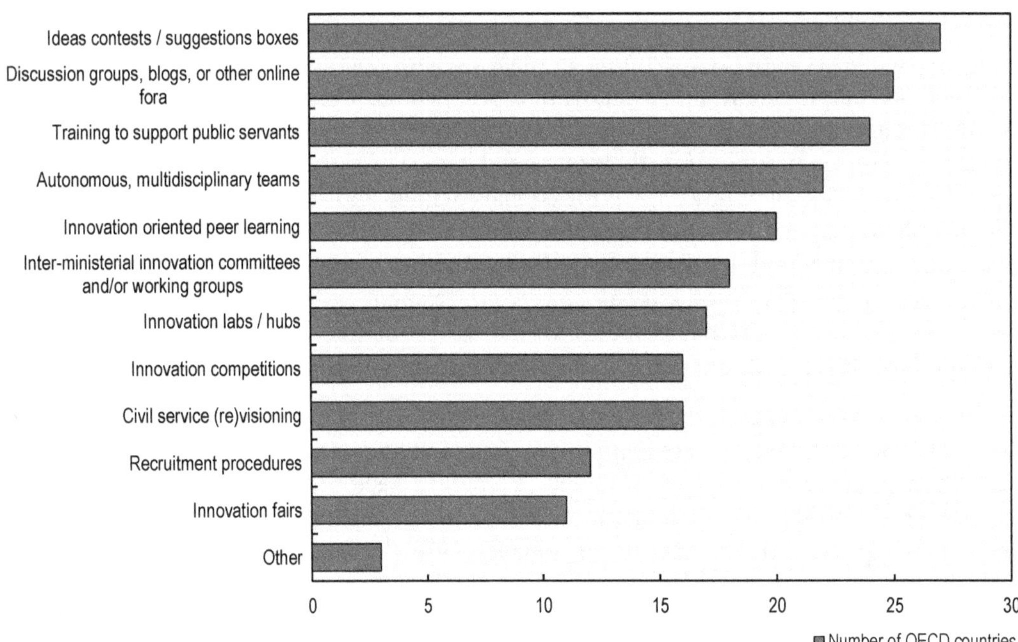

Source: 2016 Survey on Strategic Human Resource Management in Central/Federal Governments of OECD Countries

In OECD countries, training is one of the main tools currently being explored to support public sector innovation (Figure 2.4), however this training takes many forms as public sector innovation involves different combinations of skill sets. For example, a number of public service schools are designing innovation programmes for senior management which removes them from their day-to-day managerial responsibilities, builds their network and gives them time to reflect on challenges from new perspectives. While there is no perfect formula for innovation training, the following questions may be asked of good programmes: Do they take people outside their comfort zone and ask them to look at traditional problems and work in new ways, from new perspectives, with new tools and with new partners and peers? Do they look at how innovation can address societal problems and government priorities and encourage participants to link to outcomes? Do they offer hands-on opportunities to participants to iterate through evaluation, adjustment, re-allocation, and benefits realisation? Do they create a lab-like zone where participants can test tools and skills in a safe environment? Do they focus on tools for problem solving rather than on rules and procedures? Do they address organisation and personal values? Do they combine innovation principles and practices with the common language and principles of the public sector?

In short, the foregoing suggests that training innovation demands innovative training. And training innovation will not be successful in a short workshop format, but requires a longer commitment from participants, and therefore, the various actors in their institutions. The variety of forms that public sector innovation can take suggests that learning skills for innovation should be tailored to the concrete needs of the learner (Innovation and Business Skills Australia/Australian Government, 2009). In Australia for example, the Department of Education, Employment and Workplace Relations contributed to the elaboration of a training guide based on self-directed learning, activity-based and problem-based learning as the main methods to develop selected skills profiles for innovation.

Given the context-specific reality of many innovation projects, innovation training may be best learned by blending learning types. Classroom-based learning using case studies and simulation can be reinforced by experiential learning through internships or other forms of temporary assignments. Coaching can help bring outside perspective to real world challenges faced by innovators, and online platforms can provide opportunities to access data, cases and experience beyond geographical barriers.

Israel's Civil Service Cadet Programme blends intense classroom study with developmental job placements, to build and train a management cadre that is expected to catalyse change in Israel's civil service. Each year, a group is carefully chosen to participate in a six-year programme, after which each cadet is placed in a key change-oriented leadership position in the civil service. The programme entails two years of training which combines academic experience with practical experience through practicums and rotation programmes. The cadets are then placed in two positions in Ministries where they work on reform and innovation-oriented projects, while taking part in various networking opportunities to share experience with the other cadets in other ministries and agencies. In this way, cadets are supported to put their classroom-based learning into action to create real change and are provided with opportunities to continue learning and reflecting on their job experiences.

But for innovation to take hold in Chile's civil service, learning must extend far beyond the classroom and the training programme. It needs to happen on-the-job, and be a core management responsibility. Good managers slowly stretch their employees' abilities into new areas that require new knowledge development and a growing range of skills, so that everyday work becomes an opportunity to develop, practice and refine skills. This suggests the need to develop a learning culture in the public sector. Streamlining learning into work would mean rotating staff through a variety of tasks to build their competencies, taking advantage of external conferences, partnerships, opportunities to share ideas with others, and using the performance management and assessment process as an opportunity to discuss learning needs and potential. It means giving priority to learning-by-doing and giving employees the time and space to reflect on what they do and what they need to do it better.

The Experimenta Programme: learning innovation through experience in Chile's public services

The *Laboratorio de Gobierno's Experimenta* programme takes a learn-by-doing approach to build innovation capabilities. More specifically, it helps a selected group of participants to address concrete institutional challenges by strengthening their skills related to different elements of public sector innovation such as people-centred research and design, co-creation and collaboration and integration of multiple approaches.

Box 2.4. From the GIP to *Experimenta* – learning-by-doing in innovation training

The *Experimenta* is itself the result of a learning-by-doing approach. It is the evolution of a previous programme, the GIP (*Gestion de la Innovacion en el sector Publico* - Innovation management in the public sector), which ran between 2013 and 2016. The GIP's goal was to promote a culture of innovation within public institutions by funding one-year processes aimed at generating and implementing innovative solutions that add public value to specific public services.[13]

While the programme contributed to raising many innovative ideas and to creating innovation units and teams in participating institutions, the *Laboratorio's* evaluation pointed out that often innovation remained a relatively isolated process. For example, in many cases the GIP activities were not aligned with institutional goals nor with budgetary cycles; likewise, many activities were aimed at solving internal management problems rather than at creating public value to and with citizens.

Source: Information provided by *Laboratorio de Gobierno*.

Experimenta was introduced by the *Laboratorio de Gobierno* in June 2016 and the participation is open to all public sector institutions, including public corporations and public enterprises. Institutions are invited to identify a challenge they are facing. The challenge must be directly related to the organisation's strategic goals, and be affecting the users of the service. The institution also needs to appoint a team of three to seven members who will design an innovative solution over ten months of workshops and mentorship. The *Experimenta* team brings together the *Laboratorio* and experts from the private sector and civil society, who co-ordinate and help implement each of the four modules: Challenge discovery; Ideas Generation; Prototyping and testing; Managing public sector innovation, and a cross-plan of Train of trainers.[14] The working model is inspired by people-centred design, co-creation, collaboration, integration of multiple perspectives and a positive bias into experimentation.

Box 2.5. Participants in *Experimenta* round 1

In the first version, the following institutions were selected to address important challenges that were limiting their abilities to meet their strategic objectives. Through a ten-month process of coaching, mentorship and training, teams of three to seven public employees learn methods and tools to innovate and improve actual problems they face in real time.

1. *Servicio de Salud Metropolitano Oriente* (Metropolitan Health Service): Addressing the loss of specialty medical care at Red Oriente hospitals that provide care for adults and older adults.
2. *Registro Civil e Identificación* (National Register Office): Increasing Citizens' awareness and use of available channels of service to reduce unnecessary in-person visits and waiting times for services that could be obtained directly from the website.
3. *Ministerio del Deporte* (Ministry of Sports): Addressing barriers faced by beneficiaries to access and use the sports facilities in order to satisfy their demands to practice a physical activity and sport.
4. *Tesorería General de la República* (General Treasury of the Republic): Addressing user dissatisfaction with the service due to waiting times.
5. *Municipalidad de Providencia* (Municipality of Providencia): Addressing difficulties for older adults, to have collaboration networks, access to information and involvement with support services.
6. *Municipalidad de Peñalolén* (Municipality of Peñalolén): Improving opportunities to co-design Public Space, to involve the different groups of the community and generate democratic and representative decision-making processes.
7. *Corporación Nacional Forestal CONAF* (National Forest Corporation): Redesigning the tourist model to better support the National System of Protected Areas of the State (SNASPE), and increase the capacity for the conservation of the natural and cultural heritage of the Nation.
8. *SEREMI Vivienda y Urbanismo* (Regional Ministerial Office of Housing and Urbanism): Designing tools for urban development that adequately consider all the effects on people and the territory, connecting to the objectives of social integration and sustainability.
9. *Servicio Médico Legal Bío Bío* (Coroner's National Service): Improving the consideration of the emotional and situational needs of the user in addition to the technical aspects which are currently the main focus.
10. *Hospital de Talca* (Talca Hospital): Reducing waiting times for users to receive care in the Hospital Emergency Unit, Current waiting times cause deterioration in patients' health, family stress and prolonged absence from their daily activities.
11. *Municipalidad de Hualqui* (Municipality of Hualqui - Family Medical Attention Service): Improving management and access to preventive information in urban and rural healthcare users in Primary Healthcare.
12. *Dirección de Crédito Prendario* (Public Prawn Broker): Addressing the high number of items that are not redeemed by users by the corresponding deadlines so they have to be auctioned.

Source: Information provided by *Laboratorio de Gobierno*.

As the *Experimenta* programme is very new, it cannot yet identify any impact. Consequently, it will be important for the *Laboratorio* to ensure that it is collecting the right data and information about the programme to measure its impact on participants and in the participating institutions. Collecting the right training impact indicators from the start can help to ensure that the programme is on track to meeting its objectives and provide opportunities for course correction along the way. Considering the complexity of measuring public sector outcomes and public sector innovation,[15] evaluating the impact of *Experimenta* could be inspired by the 4 levels of the updated Kirkpatrick Training Evaluation Model.[16] This could involve surveying both participants and their institutions (which could be represented by the senior manager) in order to compare individual and organisational perspectives about the impact of the *Experimenta.* The surveys could be conducted immediately after the programme ends to capture the immediate impact of *Experimenta* in participants and institutions (such as the skills acquired, the time spent in the programme; in addition, a few months after the end of the programme, in order to access to what extent participants were able to apply what they learned in their work, which results did it produce and, in case participants left the institution, if they had been able to transfer the skills acquired into other institutions).

Developing innovators in the broader public service: the role of Management Improvement Programmes

Skills for innovation can also be developed within the regular training opportunities for civil servants. Similarly to the recruitment system for the public sector, the development of public employees' competencies is also determined at institutional level. Public institutions in the State's Central Administration are required[17] to develop and implement their own Staff Development Strategies (*Politica de desarollo de personas*), in collaboration with workers' associations.

In this framework, each organisation within the central public administration is responsible for identifying current and future training needs and producing an organisational learning plan including an initial training programme for civil servants (excluding SES). This relative institutional autonomy implies that getting the buy-in of public institutions regarding the need to develop skills for PSI is a key element to improve this skills' profile.

In Chile, while investment in training and staff development appears to have increased since 2003, training directly related to Public Sector Innovation is rare and fragmented across institutions. Data from SISPUBLI, an online platform used to collect data at central level about training in public services, shows that out of the 12 000 trainings programmes organised in 2014 only 59 were linked to innovation, and were mainly organised by direct client services (suggesting that the direct relationship frontline institutions have with citizens could be a trigger for a more innovative bottom-up approach). More training, without checking for quality, will not necessarily result in a more innovative civil service. Nevertheless, such a low use of training programmes to support innovation suggests that there may be opportunities to identify high-quality innovation training programmes and to replicate them more widely throughout the system.

In this framework, one important tool to improve Chile's public organisations to prepare better staff development strategies and plans has been the Management Improvement Programme "*PMG Capacitacion*" (*Programa de Mejoramiento de la Gestión*), managed by the DNSC. PMG's are thematic programmes aiming at supporting better management in the public sector by creating a system of incentives to strengthen cross-cutting key areas in public management according to a set standard. In addition to the *PMG Capacitation* which covers capacity building, other PMGs cover topics such as performance management systems, electronic government, improvement of services to users, public procurement and gender.

For each key area, PMG's define 2 levels: the basic level includes achieving targets in terms of implementing essential systems for efficient and transparent management in these areas; and the advanced level aims at creating incentives for organisations to comply with the International Standard ISO 9001:2000 for Quality management systems. Institutions benchmark themselves against a set of previously determined indicators. For example in the *PMG Capacitacion 2016*, one of the indicators is "percentage of training activities followed by an evaluation of the transferability of new skills for the job occupied by the employee".

PMGs intend to support better management in the public sector by creating a system of incentives to strengthen cross-cutting key areas in public management according with a given standard. PMG's are translated into Collective Performance Agreements (*Convenios de Desempeño Colectivo*), and whenever institutions which commit with the PMG system achieve at least 90% of the objectives, their employees receive a bonus of 5% of their salary, and for institutions that achieve between 75-90% of their objectives, employees receive a 2.5% bonus.

The main role of the DNSC within *PMG Capacitacion* is to support public institutions who participate in the programme (126 services in 2015)[18] throughout the process of improving different elements of training cycle management. Although the DNSC has no control over the training topics chosen, it provides support on training needs analysis, planning, implementation and impact evaluation of the institution's Annual Training Plan. On their side, public institutions involved in the PMG undertake to participate actively in the programme, to collaborate with the DNSC in monitoring and following up activities, implement the actions defined in the work plan, systematise and provide information about their experience.

In practice, the DNSC uses its three-year training strategy (*Estrategia de Planificacion trienal de capacitation*, the ongoing strategy in 2016-2018)[19] and a Practical Guide(2014)[20] which presents the process of training needs analysis, planning, implementation and evaluation of training, in order to help institutions design their annual training plans.

In this context, although currently none of these documents makes any reference to public sector innovation, they can be powerful instruments to communicate about PSI and to help institutions develop relevant skills. The inclusion of innovation in future editions of these documents could create the space for institutions to make more use of training programmes to develop skills to better support innovation. In particular, considering the progress in the area of public sector innovation since the launch of these documents, their next edition could include a section on skill sets for innovation and related tools to identify skills' gaps and develop skills, which could be inspired from the emerging innovation skills model introduced in the beginning of this Chapter. To use this opportunity to obtain institutional support, the DNSC could involve staff and members of the Board of the *Laboratorio* and HR professionals from institutions who have been involved in *PMG Capacitacion* in the preparation of the future editions of the Training Strategy and Practical Guide.

Streamlining and standardising innovation training across the public administration

But innovation could also be more embedded in the *PMG Capacitacion* in particular, and in training in general, if training for innovation became more comprehensive and accessible across the civil service; this could be done in three complementary ways. First, the *Laboratorio* or the DNSC could compile a database with information about potential training providers, which could include the training topics, evaluation and impact in the institution and participants. Eventually SISPUBLI could be used to extract and share a list of training programmes which could inspire institutions. The information about the quality and impact of the training would also support DNSC's strategy to promote the quality and impact of training in the public sector.

Second, this analysis of training offerings and training needs, through tools such as the survey discussed in Box 2.3, could be used to develop a basic training module on skills for innovation. This module, which could be developed by the Lab, could include guidelines for trainers following the example of the Guide created by the Australian Government and Innovation and Skills Australia (2009) and be shared on a free-to-use basis. The team in charge of preparing this module could also develop case studies inspired from innovations that won or were shortlisted for public innovation awards in Chile or abroad.

Finally, it could also be envisaged to make better[21] use of framework contracts (*Convenio Marco*) to select potential training providers for innovation related skills, as on the one hand it could simplify procedures for public institutions to organise training programmes for PSI (especially those less familiar with training for innovation) and, on the other hand, it could strengthen the implementation of a common approach of skills for innovation across different public institutions.

Ensuring the quality of innovation training

Investing in the development of skills for innovation either through programmes like *Experimenta* or in a decentralised manner raises a challenge about ensuring the quality of the training and its impact – and the DNSC made monitoring and evaluation of training investment one of its priorities. While the quality of centralised training, through *Experimenta* or even of training providers through the DNSC may find it easier to evaluate *Convenio Marco*, this may not be the case with training given by other training providers.

In this regard, it could be useful to develop some mechanism to certify the training programmes provided. France for example has created a label "School of Management and Human Resources", which consists in the certification, by a Committee of independent experts, of training programmes which are either inter-ministerial or relevant for several ministries.[22]

Another possibility in the area of certification would be to develop a system to formally recognize skills for innovation, which could be inspired from the National System of Certification of Working Competencies (*Sistema Nacional de Certificación de Competencias Laborales*) and *Chile Valora.*

Using mobility to build multidisciplinary teams and make the best use of innovation skills

Another approach to develop and spread innovation-related skills across the civil service is to support the mobility of public servants, both within and across sectors. Giving employees and leaders opportunities to work outside of their home organisation can offer opportunities to develop new insights and build new skills by giving the individual a more horizontal understanding of policy issues and allowing them to look at things from outside their sector perspective. Mobility can also increase the exchange of ideas and problem solving approaches. Mobility programs can be used to place public sector employees in other organisations for a limited time, ultimately benefiting the home organisation when the employee returns with new ideas and experiences. They can also be used to bring employees into public sector organisations from other organisations or other sectors, with competencies and perspectives developed elsewhere.

Mobility therefor can help to build multidisciplinary teams to drive innovation. The importance of building and managing multidisciplinary teams is consistently brought up in ongoing OECD research with public innovators across the OECD, including Chile. Mixed teams in terms of skills (including technical and softer skills) and backgrounds are essential for the success of innovation projects. Here profiles such as data scientists, IT and Web specialist, software engineers and legal skills are combined with equally important capabilities such as the ability to communication well and advise senior officials, knowledge of how the public administration works (which is both a soft and technical skill) and profiles such as philosophers and psychologists. This is not surprising since diversity in teams has been shown to correlate with innovation. Diversity can lead to more friction and conflict, which, if managed constructively, can lead to more creative outcomes.

Temporary teams, pilot projects and short-term assignments are all ways for governments to experiment and better align talent and resources to encourage dialogue, experimentation, risk-taking, problem-solving and innovation. OECD countries are increasingly recognising the important contribution multi-disciplinary and autonomous teams make on innovation in the public sector. Data from the OECD strategic HRM survey shows that a majority of OECD governments are experimenting with the use of autonomous, multi-disciplinary teams as a way to tap into the innovation potential of their workforce. OECD experience – which has been further supported by the findings in this review – shows that innovative projects are often spurred by work done within multi-disciplinary teams and in partnership with citizens and users (see section below). The way people are organised into teams, sometimes bridging organisational and sectoral boundaries is likely to have an influence in developing innovative capacity within the workforce.

While in the OECD countries innovation is the second most commonly stated objective of mobility programmes (see Figure 2.5), so far in Chile there are no specific programmes to encourage mobility (OECD 2016 SHRM). Currently in Chile, the capacity for horizontal mobility in the public sector is limited, meaning there is difficulty in building teams that draw on capacities in different public institutions. Currently, there is no regulatory framework that allows public officials to move from one institution to another, unless they apply for a new job in another public institution. This limits opportunities to flexibly bring together multi-disciplinary teams from different organisations for an immediate innovation project that may cross the boundaries of two organisations.

Figure 2.5. Stated objectives of mobility programmes in the civil service (2016)

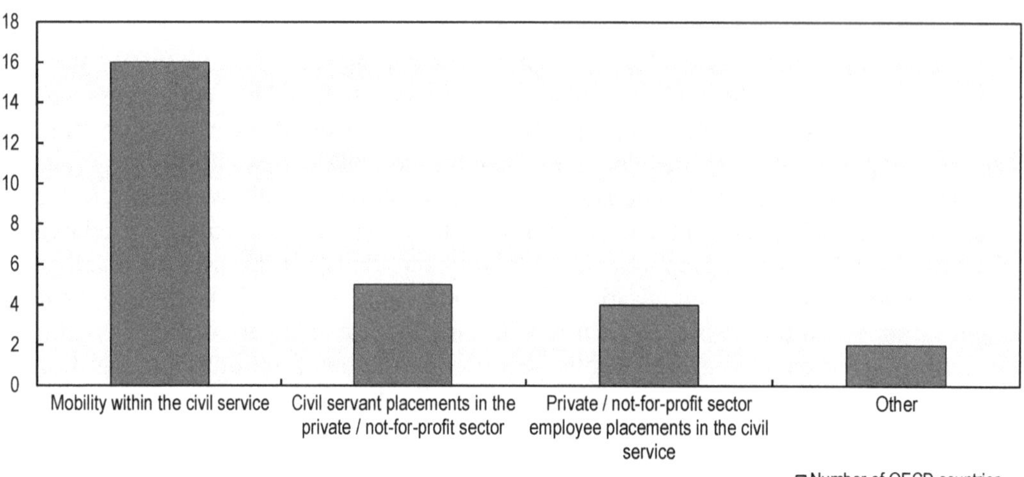

Source: 2016 Survey on Strategic Human Resource Management in Central/Federal Governments of OECD Countries.

Mobility periods in various public organisations or in the *Laboratorio*, could be used to raise awareness about innovation and facilitate communication among different services. Another advantage of such programmes could be to support replication of public innovations, if employees who were involved in successful innovation could temporarily move to a similar public institution, are interested in adapting the process, and help the team and the manager achieve it.

In addition, these thematic mobility periods would align with Law No. 20.955/2016 and the plans of the DNSC to increase mobility within the civil service. DNSC could benefit from international experience in the area of mobility programmes: Denmark organises intensive internships to learn how other public workplaces go about carrying out their tasks, and identify the best circumstances for the diffusion of innovation by organising preparatory and follow-up workshops. Canada has created Interchange Canada, a mechanism to facilitate mobility and temporary skills exchange between the Government and all other sectors of the economy, domestically and internationally, with the purpose of facilitating the transfer of knowledge, acquire specialised expertise and/or support professional development. New Zealand uses secondments within the senior leadership group as a way to promote exchange of ideas, building new relationships and broadening perspectives.[23] The USA has created the Presidential Innovation Fellows (PIF) programme which pairs top civil-servants and change makers at the highest levels of the federal government with private-sector innovators to work together for 12 months on major challenges in the areas of health, public efficiency, job creation and building a culture of innovation within the public sector[24] (Box 2.6).

Box 2.6. Developing innovation skills through mobility and internships

Canada: Interchange Policy

Interchange Canada is a mechanism to facilitate mobility and temporary exchange of skills between the Government of Canada and all other sectors of the economy, domestically and internationally. Assignments are for the purpose of knowledge-transfer, acquiring specialised expertise, and/or professional development. The Interchange Canada Policy has been used to facilitate movement between the federal government and provinces or territories, private business, non-profit organisations, academia, and indigenous organisations both within Canada and internationally.

Interchange assignments can be used to develop leadership competencies through the use of assignments to organisations where specific experience could bridge the skills-building gap. In addition, Interchange Canada can serve as an excellent means of temporarily attaining skills unavailable in the home organisation and for building and transferring knowledge to enhance internal capacity both within government and in other sectors. Furthermore, Interchange Canada directly supports several government priorities such as recruiting mobile young professionals, attracting mid-career specialists, and increasing interaction with non-government organisations.

Denmark: National innovation internship

The first national innovation internship was organised by Denmark's National Centre for Public Sector Innovation (COI) in September 2015 and the second took place in September 2016. Knowing that innovation is best diffused through the personal meeting, the national innovation internship works as an infrastructure for organising these personal meetings. In 2015 nearly 100 employees at all levels of government participated in internships lasting 2-5 days with the aim of intensively learning how other public workplaces go about carrying out their tasks. Aside from pairing, COI's focus has been on creating the best circumstances for the diffusion of innovation by organising preparatory and follow-up workshops increase the likelihood of genuinely changed behaviour and for innovative solutions to find new breeding grounds. The national innovation internship is evaluated by KORA (the Danish Institute for Local and Regional Government Research), with the aim of improving the 2016 internship. Scaling the concept is of utmost importance, as the demand for participating in 2016 has already materialised.

United States: Presidential Innovation Fellows

The Presidential Innovation Fellows (PIF) programme brings the principles, values, and practices of the innovation economy into government through the most effective agents of change we know: our people. This highly-competitive programme pairs talented, diverse technologists and innovators with top civil-servants and change-makers working at the highest levels of the federal government to tackle some our nation's biggest challenges. These teams of government experts and private-sector doers take a user-centric approach to issues at the intersection of people, processes, products, and policy to achieve lasting impact.

Fellows selected for this unique, and highly-competitive opportunity serve for 12 months, during which they will collaborate with each other and federal agency partners on high-profile initiatives aimed at saving lives, saving taxpayers' money, fuelling job creation, and building the culture of entrepreneurship and innovation within government.

Sources: Information provided by the Canadian PEM delegate; Center for Offentlig Innovation, Innovationspraktik, www.coi.dk/hovedaktiviteter/innovationspraktik; Presidential Innovation Fellows, https://presidentialinnovationfellows.gov/.

In Chile, based on the survey data and examples collected in interviews during the fact-finding mission, there is some use of multidisciplinary teams to spur innovation and to implement innovation projects. One such example comes from the Ministry of Transport Smart Cities Unit, which brought together a multidisciplinary team including engineers, philosophers, informatics experts, and architects, to work collaboratively with actors inside and outside government to redesign services and improve the mobility of cities.

To scale up these practices two things should be considered. First, how do the current structure and channels function in the public sector to allow for the building of such multidisciplinary teams? Secondly, on an organisational but also on a government-wide level, it would be helpful if the reserve of skills and talent could be tracked within and from one organisation to another. Being able to identify people with the right talents within an organisation would be a first step to building the kinds of multidisciplinary teams required to support innovation. This would imply the need for a skills inventory related to innovation.

As DNSC's Practical Guide puts it, training is a key tool for managing people, but will only be useful if its objectives are aligned with the organisational strategy. This has two implications. First, it means that while training is a key element to develop skills, it is not an end in itself. In this perspective, skills acquired through training should be put into practice in the workplace – and even the best of training programmes may be pointless if organisations fail to create the space to put the new skills into practice.

Second, more than training, institutions need to create additional learning opportunities. As presented above, mobility is one of such opportunities, and many others can be implemented in the public sector. They can include for example programmes such as mentoring, but also the development of incentives and challenges to motivate employees to innovate, such as the creation of innovation awards or support to innovators networks, which will be explained in more detail in the next chapter.

Conclusion and recommendations

On recruiting:

- Building a skilled workforce is the first step to support public sector innovation in a sustainable way. With regard to recruitment, the DNSC could include the concept of Public Sector Innovation and innovation skills in the preparation of the *Plan de Asesorias en Reclutamiento y seleccion*. To support buy-in at institutional level, it could also involve selection committees and HR professionals in the development and piloting of the Plan. The involvement of these professionals would strengthen their ownership of the Plan and could lead to a more effective implementation. The pilot group could form a multi-organisational task force to raise awareness about skills for innovation and explore the idea of developing a more formal innovation framework for recruitment, which could involve additional institutions.
- Another possibility in this area would be for the DNSC to further develop the concept of skills for innovation in the *Manual Seleccion de Personas en servicios publicos*, specifying the different roles expected of public employees (civil servants and contrata) and middle managers. Training could be provided to members of selection committees to better identify and recruit skills for public sector innovation.

- Recruiting innovators also implies being able to attract them. The DNSC could highlight all the activities (awards, training, projects) related to PSI on the website used to advertise public employment, in the internship programme in public administration managed by the DNSC and in all relevant communication tools to attract future civil servants.

On developing skills for public sector innovation

- In parallel with recruitment for innovation, developing skills for innovation in Chile can be done through regular training programmes and through innovation-specific programmes. The use of regular training programmes to develop innovation-related skills is still very limited. The DNSC could potentially use tools like Sispubli to collect additional data on the development of skills for innovation, for example about the types of skills that are being developed, the training providers, the methodologies, the participants, or the evaluation of the training programmes. In addition to the collection and centralisation of data, a *Convenio Marco* could be used to select training providers to contribute to the strategic development of training for innovation and be used to measure the interest in such training.
- In addition to regular training programmes, the *Laboratorio* has created the programme *Experimenta* to develop innovation skills in a selected group of public employees. This programme has great potential to raise awareness about innovation and to develop civil servants' skills for innovation and the ability to measure the impact of *Experimenta* will be a key aspect for the sustainability of public sector innovation in Chile. The *Laboratorio* could start by focusing on the impact of the programme on the participants and their institutions. The *Laboratorio* could conduct surveys to monitor and measure the impact of *Experimenta*, during and after the programme. In addition to participants, their managers (current and future, including in case of transfers to other institutions) could be surveyed as well to measure the change produced by *Experimenta* in the participant institutions.
- With regard to the variety of training methods, programmes and providers, it could be envisaged to create a certification programme for skills for innovation, which could be inspired by Chile *Valora*. The *Laboratorio de Gobierno* and the DNSC could work together to develop such certification.

Notes

1 http://innovation.govspace.gov.au/barriers/#g.

2 http://innovation.govspace.gov.au/barriers/#g.

3 https://www.whitehouse.gov/sites/default/files/strategy_for_american_innovation_october_2015.pdf.

4 www.fonction-publique.gouv.fr/reunions-bilaterales-de-strategie-de-modernisation-rh.

5 www.cpsa.ie/en/About-Us/What-we-do/Setting-Recruitment-Standards/Code-of-Practice-for-Atypical-Appointments-to-Positions-in-the-Civil-Service-and-Certain-Public-Bodies.pdf.

6 Which corresponds to a coverage rate of 77% of civil servants in 2012.

7 www.serviciocivil.gob.cl/ip_bpl.

8 www.empleospublicos.cl.

9 www.bloomberg.org/program/government-innovation/#innovation-teams.

10 www.livingcities.org/work/innovation-teams/about.

11 www.practicasparachile.cl.

12 http://polisci.msu.edu/index.php/undergraduate-program/internship-program/innovategov and https://msumpp.wordpress.com/2016/09/27/innovategov-service-learning-internship-featuring-elizabeth-raczkowski/.

13 The criteria for allocating the fund were: Suitability of the Expert Institution, Approval of the preliminary investigation, exploration suitability of users, level of commitment of public institution, Public value proposition delivering the project, quality of the technical proposal and relevance of the requested budget.

14 www.estadoinnovador.cl/#en-que-consiste.

15 Namely due to the diverse nature of the services, the wide range of users, the difficulties in defining targets (see literature review in Kattel et al., 2013).

16 The four levels are 1) Reaction: The degree to which participants find the training favourable, engaging and relevant to their jobs; 2) Learning: The degree to which participants acquire the intended knowledge, skills, attitude, confidence and commitment based on their participation in the training; 3) Behaviour: The degree to which participants apply what they learned during training when they return to workand 4) Results: The degree to which targeted outcomes are achieved as a result of the training, support and accountability package (www.kirkpatrickpartners.com/OurPhilosophy/TheNewWorldKirkpatrickModel/tabid/303/Default.aspx).

17 Presidential Instruction No. 001/2015 on Good Labour Practices in Staff Development in the State.

18 www.sispubli.cl/wp-content/uploads/2014/11/Listado-Servicios-PAC-2015.xlsx.

19 Strategy available here: http://www.sispubli.cl/wp-content/uploads/2015/10/DOCUMENTO-ESTRETEGIA-DE-CAPACITACION-2016-2018.doc

20 Practical guide available here: www.serviciocivil.gob.cl/sites/default/files/guia_practica_gestionar_capacitacion_servicios_publicos_2014.pdf

21 Current providers of training for public sector innovation are Universities, technical training centres, training organisations, some public services and consultants who are selected through framework contracts in *ChileCompra* (*Convenio Marco*).

22 www.fonction-publique.gouv.fr/labellisation-des-formations-de-lecole-management-et-des-rh/

23 www.ssc.govt.nz/mobility-senior-leadership-and-management.

24 https://presidentialinnovationfellows.gov.

References

Borins, Sandford (2002), "Leadership and innovation in the public sector", in *Leadership & Organization Development Journal*, 23/8, pp. 467-476.

Center for Offentlig Innovation, Innovationspraktik, www.coi.dk/hovedaktiviteter/innovationspraktik

DIPRES (2015), Estadísticas de Recursos Humanos del Sector Público 2005-2014, Publicación de la Dirección de Presupuestos del Ministerio de Hacienda, available in www.dipres.gob.cl/572/articles-140439_doc_pdf.pdf

Dyer, Jeff, Hal Gregerson, Clayton M. Christensen (2011), "The Innovator's DNA: Mastering the Five Skills of Disruptive Innovators", *Boston: Harvard Business Review Press*.

Innovation & Business Skills Australia/Australian Government (2009), "Developing innovation skills: A Guide for trainers and assessors to foster the innovation skills of learners through professional practice", available at www.ibsa.org.au/sites/default/files /downloads/CP-INN01.pdf.

Katel et al. (2013), "Can we measure public sector innovation?" *A literature review*, LIPSE Project paper, available at http://lipse.org/userfiles/uploads/kattel%20et%20al %20egpa%20version.pdf.

OECD (2017, forthcoming), Core skills for public sector innovation: a model of skills to promote and enable innovation in public sector organisations.

OECD (2017, forthcoming), Fostering Innovation in the Public Sector.

OECD (2016), *Engaging Public Employees for a High-Performing Civil Service*, OECD Public Governance Reviews, OECD Publishing, Paris, http://dx.doi.org/10.1787/9789264267190-en

OECD (2015), *The Innovation Imperative in the Public Sector: Setting an Agenda for Action*, OECD Publishing, Paris. http://dx.doi.org/10.1787/9789264236561-en.

OECD (2011), *Skills for Innovation and Research*, OECD Publishing, Paris, http://dx.doi.org/10.1787/9789264097490-en.

OECD (2010), *Innovative Workplaces: Making Better Use of Skills within Organisations*, OECD Publishing, Paris, http://dx.doi.org/10.1787/9789264095687-en.

Presidential Innovation Fellows, https://presidentialinnovationfellows.gov/.

Chapter 3.

Motivating Chilean public employees to innovate

This chapter discusses the ways that Chilean civil servants are motivated to contribute to innovation. Motivation can be intrinsic or extrinsic and can be encouraged or discouraged by management practices, rewards and recognition and by organisational culture. The chapter suggests the need to understand organisational culture as both a cause and effect of public sector innovation and suggests opportunities to measure and benchmark elements of organisational culture through the use of employee surveys. The use of innovation awards are one important tool that is used in Chile to build a more innovation oriented organisational culture. Suggestions are made to make more use of the innovation cases that are submitted to the award in order to share ideas and inspire new ones. Chile has also taken steps to develop an innovator's network and suggestions are given to maximise the potential of this group.

Building the innovation-oriented skills and capacities of Chile's public sector workforce alone will not contribute to increasing and improving public sector innovation without ensuring that the workforce is both motivated to do so, and has the opportunity to do so. In some ways motivation can make up for lack of skill as highly motivated people will be more likely to transfer skills from other domains, or invest more effort in acquiring the necessary skills (Amabile, 1997). This chapter will look at ways that public organisations can motivate civil servants to innovate, and support civil servants who are already motivated.

Motivation is a key input to a wide range of performance outcomes at a personal and organisational level. As with skills and abilities, motivation can be thought of both in terms of individuals, as an element of one's personality, but also in an organisational and relational sense – people can be motivated to do things when inspired to do so by others. Motivation is therefore a variable state that can be influenced, and work motivation can be influenced by a range of elements such as the work environment, task design, organisational culture and the relationship between an employee and their line manager. Even if the employee has all the abilities required to perform, they will only use them if it is recognised by the organisation. Hence, organisations must offer the right incentives to motivate the best behaviour (Boxall and Purcell, 2011).

It's important to distinguish between intrinsic and extrinsic motivation. Intrinsic motivation compels people to act for a reward that is gained from the act itself, possibly because it brings them pleasure, a sense of personal satisfaction or pride, or because it conforms to their own standards (e.g. values-based standards, such as community service, commitment to family, and ethical fairness). Extrinsic motivation compels people to act for a reward that is separate from the act itself. The most common example is financial payment for services rendered.

Box 3.1. Amabile's componential theory of creativity

The Componential Theory of Creativity, and the research that underlies it, suggest a number of management implications concerning the motivation for creativity in business and the effect of the work environment on that motivation.

- Because human motivation is so complex and so important, the successful management of creativity for the next century must include management education about the types of motivation, their sources, their effects on performance, and their susceptibility to various work environment influences.
- We cannot hope to create a highly and appropriately creative workforce simply by "loading up" the intrinsic and the extrinsic motivators in the work environment, without paying attention to the type of extrinsic motivators and the context in which they are presented.
- Because a positive sense of challenge in the work is one of the most important predictors of creativity, it is imperative to match people to work that utilizes their skills, stretches their skills, and is clearly valued by the organisation. As much as possible, all work should be designed to maximize intrinsically motivating aspects.
- Organisations must demonstrate a strong orientation toward innovation, which is clearly communicated and enacted, from the highest levels of management, throughout the organisation.

Box 3.1. Amabile's componential theory of creativity *(continued)*

- Organisations should orient themselves toward the generation, communication, careful consideration, and development of new ideas. This includes fair, constructive judgment of ideas, non-controlling reward and recognition for creative work, mechanisms for developing new ideas, and an active flow of ideas. It excludes turf battles, conservatism, and excessively negative criticism of new ideas.
- Work groups should be constituted of diversely skilled individuals with a shared intrinsic motivation for their work and a willingness to both share and constructively criticize each other's ideas. These groups should be led by supervisors who clearly set overall goals for projects but allow operational autonomy in achieving those goals. Performance feedback should be highly informational and work-focused.
- People should be given at least adequate resources to carry out their work, and at least minimally sufficient time to consider alternative approaches.

Source: Amabile, Teresa M (1997), "Motivating Creativity in Organisations: On Doing what you Love and Loving what you Do", *California Management Review*, Fall 1997, 40, 1.

Research often concludes that intrinsic motivation is more useful for motivating creativity and innovation than extrinsic motivation. While some individuals may arrive at a job with a higher degree of intrinsic motivation than others, this motivation can be nurtured or smothered by organisational surroundings (for an overview see Mumford, 2000). For example some (Amabile, 1997; Fernandez and Moldogaziev, 2012) suggest that extrinsic motivation, especially in the form of rewards for short-term performance, can result in a narrower view of the task and can cause employees to avoid innovative ways of doing things.

According to Foss et al (2009), work can be designed in a way that builds intrinsic motivation. First, the work must be perceived as meaningful by the employee and this can be done by giving them responsibility for a full project as opposed to contributing one small piece. The level of responsibility and autonomy given to the employee is related. The more autonomy, the more personal responsibility people are given for the outcomes, the more motivated they will be to complete the job well. The third element is feedback. Direct and clear performance-relevant information received as the task is carried out can motivate. This can be both inherent in the job, as could be the case of a teacher who sees their students improve, or it could be externally through their manager or stakeholder community.

Extrinsic motivation does not necessarily need to limit intrinsic motivation. Some forms of extrinsic motivation are shown to increase intrinsic motivation and creativity; these are reward and recognition for creative ideas, well-defined project goals, and frequent, constructive feedback.

This chapter will look at the motivation of Chilean civil servants through an organisational lens, beginning first with a consideration of organisational culture in Chile's civil service. This is followed by a discussion of specific tools that are increasingly being used to support civil servants' motivation to contribute to innovation: innovation awards, and innovation networks.

Assessment of motivation for public sector innovation in Chile

The public employees who participated in interviews and workshops as part of this review demonstrated a very high level of motivation to contribute to innovation and to improve the services they provide to citizens. It is clear that this group of public employees are driven by a strong personal commitment to the work they do, take great pride in the services they provide, and are intrinsically motivated to improve the lives of Chile's citizens through better and more innovative service delivery. Often, however, this motivation is dampened by a bureaucratic system that is perceived to be overly rigid and legalistic. Most innovators spoke of organisational cultures that favour compliance to the existing laws over creative problem solving. Innovators often painted a picture of isolation, frustration with the slow pace of acceptance of ideas and lack of support from management and peers.

It must be noted, however, that the employees with whom the teams met were all associated in some way with the *Laboratorio de Gobierno*, which played a key role in identifying participants. These employees' perception of the level of motivation among their colleagues in their organisation tended to be mixed. Some perceived a lot of motivation amongst their peers that needed to be supported and directed. They spoke of oversubscription to innovation training and events, and an enthusiasm to learn about alternative ways of approaching problems and new tools to help them achieve their objectives. Others perceived low levels of motivation amongst most public employees due primarily to a lack of incentive structures that reward innovative behaviour and the impression that most public employees were overworked and had little time to invest in innovation efforts.

Many of the interviewees pointed out that most Chilean public employees do not associate the concept of innovation with the kind of work they do. They suggested that Chilean public employees still associate innovation with large scale IT reforms, and not with service-oriented improvements that they have been involved in. This point was illustrated with reference to the *Funciona!* innovation award (discussed in more detail below), for which few applied despite the existence of much innovation. Creating a network of co-ordinators who were responsible for promoting the award helped to make civil servants realise that they were involved in innovation. Once clearly articulated, applications for the prize increased significantly. Others spoke of their surprise at the amount of interest in innovation training once they had explained what it entailed. Clarifying the concept and showing employees that innovation is happening in public services can be an important step to motivating employees to do more of it.

Some suggested higher levels of motivation at lower levels of the hierarchy, with more resistance at the middle management level. This is also reflected in the pilot survey that was carried out with the group of 20 innovators discussed in the previous chapter (Box 2.3). In all skills areas, except data literacy, this group of innovation-oriented public employees rated their manager's support for using their skills as significantly lower than their own abilities. In fact, there was generally a very small gap between their manager's support and their organisation's readiness, suggesting that their relationship with their line managers is impeding their motivation to put their skills to use. While the sample size of the pilot exercise cannot lend itself to broader generalisations, the tool could be used more extensively within and across particular public organisations to assess where managers are providing motivation and thereby identify good practices that can be shared with others. The importance of good management is addressed more thoroughly in Chapter 4.

Organisational culture: The unwritten barriers to innovating in Chile

Organisational culture is made up of "core values, behavioural norms, artefacts and behavioural patterns which govern the way people in an organisation interact with each other and invest their energy in their jobs and the organisation at large" (Gee and Miles, 2008). Organisational culture can be thought of as the unspoken rules and values which exist in the heads and hearts of the employees and managers who make up the organisation. Culture is not something written in regulation, policy or employee handbooks, and as such it hard to identify and hard to change, but nevertheless highly important.

An innovation-oriented organisational culture would mean that employees see themselves as potential innovators, and expect that the time and effort they devote to innovation-oriented activity would be valued and rewarded. In such an organisation employees would be able to point to innovations their organisation has contributed to, and see the career advancement of those who lead innovations. Furthermore, employees would expect to be given space to come up with new ideas and have these ideas taken seriously, even if they did not result in innovation.

In Chile, the general perception is that organisational culture is not generally supportive of innovation in the public sector. Participants, in interviews and workshops pointed to low risk acceptance, low levels of collaboration and trust, and fear of making mistakes as some of the cultural elements that act as barriers and de-motivate civil servants who want to innovate. These are reinforced by organisational elements, such as budgetary constraints and the complex legal and regulatory environment in which most public employees work. This can prevent innovative behaviours, and discourage people with high levels of innovative capacity and intrinsic motivation from joining or remaining in the civil service.

Developing a common vision and narrative about public sector innovation and the associated expectations about the behaviour of civil servants can contribute to creating a supportive organisational culture. In Australia for example, developing an "innovation consciousness" within the public sector is one of the key areas highlighted in the Public Sector Innovation toolkit. Its Innovation Action Plan[1] "provides a framework to embed a common understanding of what innovation means and why it is important in the public sector context". Connectivity, access to information and communication are identified as the main pillars that can support innovation consciousness.

It is increasingly possible to measure and benchmark employee's perceptions of their organisation and its culture through employee surveys. The US and the UK, for example, conduct civil service-wide employee surveys which give every employee of every organisation under the central government the opportunity to express their views. They use these surveys to develop indices around themes of employee engagement, motivation, perceptions of management and leadership, and even views on innovation. Results are calculated for the civil service as a whole, each organisation, and within the organisational units, to enable benchmarking and comparative analysis. This can be very useful to identify organisations and units that perform well and those that perform less well, and to generate cross-organisational learning (OECD, 2016).

When it comes to innovation-oriented culture, employee surveys can provide data and insight into the way employees are motivated to contribute to innovation, and where opportunities are present. In Ireland, for example, employees are asked to agree or disagree with statements related to the acceptance of new ideas in their organisation, the flexibility of their department to adapt to change and employee's motivation to contribute to improvements. In the US, three questions are combined into an innovation index which includes employees' motivation to look for better ways of doing things, and whether such motivation is encouraged and rewarded by their organisation. The UK also has a range of questions which explore the support employees sense contribute to innovation and to challenge the way things are done. Putting these questions together to create an index and benchmark organisations and even teams can help to show which organisations are succeeding at developing an innovation-oriented culture and which still have a way to go.

According to data collected by the DNSC (*Barometro de gestion de personas*, 2013) 45% of organisations in the Central Public Administration conducted surveys to measure the working climate between 2007 and 2013, although it is unclear whether these are conducted regularly. Updated data in this area would provide the DNSC with information about how many and which institutions conduct this type of regular measurements. This could be a first step towards developing a single survey for the whole civil service.

If a number of institutions conduct employee surveys on a regular basis, the DNSC could analyse the content of the surveys to see what is measured and how and analyse to what extent the data and methodology across institutions is comparable. Building on this initial analysis, the DNSC could create a survey that would either conduct itself or incorporated it into existing surveys. This could include questions related to public sector innovation, and an innovation-oriented culture (see Box 3.2 below for examples of questions related to innovation from the surveys in the US, the UK and Ireland).

The results of these questions could be used to support a more innovation-oriented management, benchmark organisations and track the effectiveness of various interventions. For example, it could help to identify areas where employees perceive a more innovation-oriented culture. Further investigation of these areas, for example, through case study analysis, could generate insights and lessons for other areas. Tracking results over time could also provide an indication of whether actions to address innovation are effective.

In the longer term, employee survey data could be analysed together with information about the effectiveness of recruitment, training and leadership policies, to detect impact and effectiveness. Collecting employee perceptions on the effectiveness of public sector innovation, HR systems and skills match are also important elements to align the existing workforce skills with long term organisational objectives.

Box 3.2. Measuring an innovative organisational culture

Ireland's Civil Service Employee Engagement survey

The Employee Engagement Survey is an important action in the Civil Service Renewal Plan, a plan focused on building on the strengths of the Civil Service and tracking what needs to improve for the future. The survey included a section to measure the innovative climate which analysed the following innovation-related questions:

- new ideas are readily accepted here
- the Department is quick to respond when changes need to be made
- management here are quick to spot the need to do things differently
- the Department is very flexible: it can quickly change procedures to meet new conditions and solve problems as they arise
- people in the Department are always searching for new ways of looking at problems.

Box 3.2. Measuring an innovative organisational culture *(continued)*

The results of the survey, first run in 2015, showed that, on average, only 45% of employees agreed with the above statements. This result shows that Ireland has some work to do to address this, and provides a useful benchmark to measure the impact of reforms in this area. Result of the full survey can be accessed here: http://www.per.gov.ie/en/civil-service-employee-engagement-survey/.

United Kingdom: Civil Service People Survey

The UK has been conducting a Civil Service People Survey (CSPS) since 2009 that which looks at civil servants' attitudes to and experience of working in government departments. The 7th annual Civil Service People Survey (2015) was conducted across 96 Civil Service organisations, including government departments, executive agencies and Crown non-departmental public bodies. The questions that relate the most to innovation are the following:

- my manager is open to my ideas
- the people in my team work together to find ways to improve the service we provide
- the people in my team are encouraged to come up with new and better ways of doing things
- I think it is safe to challenge the way things are done in [my organisation]
- I believe I would be supported if I try a new idea, even if it may not work.

USA: The Best Places to work in Federal government

The "Best Places to Work in the Federal Government" survey aims to measure employee satisfaction and commitment; the results provided managers and leaders with a way to measure and improve employee satisfaction and commitment and are an important tool for ensuring that employee satisfaction is a top priority. They provide a mechanism to hold agency leaders accountable for the health of their organisations; serve as an early warning sign for agencies in trouble; and offer a roadmap for improvement.

The survey includes three questions related to innovation:

- I feel encouraged to come up with new and better ways of doing things
- I am constantly looking for ways to do my job better
- creativity and innovation are rewarded.

Sources: Government of Ireland (2015), Civil Service Employee Engagement Survey, www.per.gov.ie/en/civil-service-employee-engagement-survey/; Government of the United Kingdom/Cabinet Office (2015), Civil Service People Survey 2015, www.gov.uk/government/uploads/system/uploads/attachment_data/file/477335/csps2015_benchmark_report.pdf and www.gov.uk/government/publications/civil-service-people-survey-2015-results; Partnership for Public Service, The Best Places to Work in the Federal Government, http://bestplacestowork.org/BPTW/rankings/categories/large/innovation.

Measurement alone is rarely enough to produce change and setting out to change organisational culture is not an easy mission. This is in part because culture can be treated as both a consequence and a cause. Changing culture then requires seeing it as a consequence of clear and consistent alignment of values, processes and behaviours. This takes time, sustained effort, and clear commitment from top and middle management.

With this in mind, survey results can be a useful tool to support culture change when they are embedded in a structured follow up process.

In the US, where an annual survey is conducted, each agency was asked to designate one senior official responsible for improving survey results. These officials work with the Office of Personnel Management to understand their agency's results. Agencies are provided with detailed breakdowns in order to pinpoint specific areas that may underperform. This enables a tailored and targeted intervention. The OPM also makes an effort to highlight organisations with the most impressive scores on the Federal Employee Viewpoint Survey (FEVS) and those with the greatest improvements over the year[2]. In 2016, the top increase in scores was achieved by the US Department of Energy, which took a multi-pronged approach to directly addressing its results (Box 3.3). This example shows how measurement through employee surveys can be used to inspire wider organisational improvements. In the case of the DOE, the goal was to improve employee engagement (an antecedent of public sector innovation, see OECD 2016) and the same approach could be applied specifically to innovation.

Box 3.3. Strengthening organisational culture at the US Department of Energy

The US Department of Energy's (DOE) scores on the Federal Employee Viewpoint Survey (FEVS) declined significantly from 2011 to 2014. In December 2014, the Administration issued a memorandum providing direction and guidance that directed agencies to strengthen employee engagement and organisational performance.[3] DOE took on this challenge using a multi-pronged approach to strengthen employee engagement.

Strategies and actions taken to address low engagement scores:

1. **Leaders set clear goals and review progress**: The Secretary and DOE senior leaders visibly communicated their commitment, expectations, and goals for strengthening employee engagement. For instance, leaders held programme-level all-hands meetings with employees within 60 days of the Secretary's Town Hall. Leaders demonstrated commitment to employee engagement goals by interacting regularly with employees in a variety of ways. Information obtained was incorporated into agency and programme action plans. This was a change from the previous top-down only approach which led to positive results. In addition, the Office of the Chief Human Capital Officer (CHCO) met programme managers to discuss successes and challenges in employee engagement, and reported progress regularly to the Secretary and Deputy Secretary.
2. **Senior Executive Service (SES) members and managers are supported and held accountable for improvement**: DOE appointed Senior Accountable Officials (SAO) to implement Administration requirements. In 2016, all SES performance plans included a measurable element, along with training and consultations, related to action planning and/or results to improve employee engagement.
3. **FEVS data is disseminated and organised for action**: DOE created a first-of-its-kind Organisational Management Report (OMR) and analysis tool to support data interpretation and action planning. In 2016, FEVS results were disseminated to 520 work units at 7 organisational levels across the Department, and in support of transparency, all reports will be made available to employees.
4. **Increased adoption of employee-driven and evidence-based practices**: The CHCO led and managed collaborations with the DOE Labor Management Forum and DOE Programme Offices to share successful practices and common engagement challenges, and implement employee-led recommendations. In addition, DOE Workplace Improvement Networks (WIN) were launched in Headquarters and Field Offices to expand the practice of employee-led workplace improvement at local levels throughout the Department.

Box 3.3. Strengthening organisational culture at the US Department of Energy *(continued)*

Measurable impact:

In 2016, DOE led all "Large Agencies" (10 000 to 74 999 federal employees) for increases in overall Engagement and all three engagement subfactors, as well as for increases in overall Inclusion and all five Habits of Inclusion. In addition, DOE's Workplace Improvement Networks have produced visible employee-driven improvements in facilities and programmes throughout the Department.

Source: OECD (2016), *Engaging Public Employees for a High-Performing Civil Service*, http://dx.doi.org/10.1787/9789264267190-en.

New Zealand's Department of Internal Affairs (DIA) employs over 2 000 people on 49 sites and fulfils one of the broadest portfolios in government with 6 Ministers and oversight of around 100 pieces of legislation. In 2012, its staff engagement score, a key indicator of a successful organisational culture, was one of the lowest in the country's public sector in 2012 (9.3% of people were engaged, 56.6% were ambivalent and 34.1% were disengaged). The arrival of a new Chief Executive supported a programme of change which included activities for staff around a common theme brought the diverse range of DIA people together. The shift in the DIA culture led to a 155% increase in engaged people from 2012 to 2015, and is now above the New Zealand public sector benchmark on key engagement drivers, including confidence in leadership.[4]

Germany's employment agency (Bundesagentur fur Arbeit – BA) also conducts a detailed employee survey that provides breakdowns for its staff of 98 000 employees across the country. After the survey is conducted, results are shared transparently through an IT-supported "Leadership Information Cockpit", which is provided by the controlling unit. BA then undertakes a structured follow-up process that involves workshops for managers to understand results, and support to develop a follow-up strategy. Workshops and support tend to focus on: dialogue-based local processes to bring local employees together with senior leaders to discuss results and concerns; opportunities for employees to contribute to continuous improvement; and discussions of well-being and health management. Furthermore, BA encourages the sharing of good engagement practices through regular network meetings and a planned "action database" with best practice examples.

Developing an innovation-oriented organisational culture could also be supported by a strong symbol such as the creation of a "Charter for Innovation". Such a Charter could be inspired by other public sector charters, for example Ireland's 2002 Customer Charter Initiative[5] that supports organisations to engage with their customers to design their services better and to become more flexible and responsive to the needs of the users of such services.

Awards and challenges to recognise innovation

Innovation challenges and awards to celebrate innovation success can reinforce an innovation-oriented organisational culture and can help diffuse innovations by enabling groups to learn from each other's experience (OECD, 2015b). Challenges and awards can also be a source of recognition for innovators which can help motivate. Finally, awards can help raise awareness about public sector innovation across the public sector and society. This section will first look at awards which recognise successful innovations in the public sector (*ex post*), and secondly at challenges that are used to source innovative solutions to problems (*ex ante*).

Awards

OECD countries use a wide range of public sector awards to recognise successful public sector innovation in different areas of the civil service: in Sweden for example, the award recognises a government agency for its efficient service, dedicated employees, innovation and a sustainable and environmentally conscious development. In the United States the Presidential Rank Awards Programme recognises a select group of career members of the Senior Executive Service (SES) for exceptional performance. In Norway the innovation award aims at sharing knowledge and inspiration about innovation within the local Public Sector. In Slovenia the award is given to the most innovative e-government solution (see Box 3.4 below for more examples).

Box 3.4. Public Sector Innovation contests and awards

Australia: Public Sector Innovation Awards

The Public Sector Innovation Awards aim at recognising, celebrating and sharing innovative approaches to public administration, and to foster a culture that supports and celebrates people and agencies across the Australian Public Service (APS). Innovations can involve one or multiple organisations regardless of their size, or level. The awards recognise initiatives in four areas: creating improved solutions to an existing problem; recognising new methods or new technologies; strengthening the culture and capability for innovation; and providing better services and facilitating interactions with citizens.

Austria: Public Sector Award as part of the Innovation Ecosystem

The National Austrian Public Sector Innovation Prize, which has been in place for over 10 years on a biannual basis, includes 4 categories: a) Leadership and Management; b) Innovative Service Design; c) Diversity, Gender and Integration; d) the forth category is dedicated to a topical challenge such as demographic change. The jury of national and international experts consists of practitioners, scientists, consultants and private sector. A special prize is awarded by students of public management studies. Best practices from the award are held in a national data-base (www.verwaltungspreis.gv.at) and shared publicly in innovation conferences and events. A number of them have also been included in the OECD's Observatory of Public Sector Innovation. Selected projects are further developed within the scope of the newly founded innovation lab "GovLab Austria".

Belgium: Mission Possible

Belgium's SPF Personnel et Organisation (SPF P&O) promoted the innovation award "Innovation, vehicle for greater efficiency" in the context of the seminar for managers "Better, with less, together, differently: mission possible" (2011). The award recognises proposals, ideas, initiatives or projects related to identifying new methods allowing the federal administration to work in a more efficient and sustainable way. Both individuals and teams from the Federal administration can participate. The innovations have to focus on one of the following topics: quality and efficiency of the services, optimisation, open innovation, culture and engagement The selection of the winning innovation was made by the managers present in the seminar "Mission Possible".

Box 3.4. Public Sector Innovation contests and awards *(continued)*

Poland: "Professionals in the service of citizens"

In 2013/14 and 2014/15 the Head of Civil Service organised two editions of the competition entitled "Professionals in the service of citizens". Its main aim was to promote modern solutions regarding customer service management applied in the government administration. The competition was expected also to:

- encourage the offices to increase customer service standards
- improve the government administration image
- build trust in the administration.

All civil service institutions, applying the mandatory standards of human resource management set by the Head of the Civil Service, were eligible to take part in the competition by sending their good practice description. The practices were assessed by the Competition Committee on the basis of the following criteria:

- creativity (degree of uniqueness and novelty)
- effectiveness (in the scope of the quality and scope of customer service)
- replicability and universality (possibility of applying a given solution in other offices).

In two editions, almost 120 good practices were submitted. The best ones were widely promoted during the Awards Ceremony and afterwards with the use of various channels of communication.

Spain: Public Management Innovation awards

Public Management Innovation awards recognise public organisations which have been distinguished in innovation practices. There are two categories:

- Citizenship's award, intended for innovative practices in products or service delivery, with an effect on citizens or users.
- Innovation in the management's award. This award is intended for initiatives orientated towards enhancing the organisation or management procedures in public organisations. Those initiatives do not have to directly affect citizens or users, but they will benefit them as a result.

Quality and Innovation in public management awards are intended to grant public organisations distinguished for their excellence in global performance, innovation in knowledge and information management as well as technologies, and quality and impact of singular improvement initiatives implemented.

There is an annual call for the Public management's excellence award, and a biennial call for Public management's innovation awards (both types).

Sources: Australia: Institute of Public Administration Australia , "Public Sector Innovation Awards", www.act.ipaa.org.au/innovation-awards; Belgium: Feb web le portail du personnel fédéral (2011), Concours Innovation, véhicule d'efficience, www.fedweb.belgium.be/sites/default/files/downloads/20110905_reglement_concours_innovation.pdf.; Poland: information provided by the PEM delegate; Spain: Directorate General for the Civil Service (Susana Mayo).

In Chile the first public sector innovation award dates back to 1999 (before the creation of the DNSC) and was managed by Segpres. Even before the creation of the *Laboratorio de Gobierno*, the DNSC was responsible for one of the main innovation projects across the civil service, *Funciona!* Award (Table 3.1).

Table 3.1. Selected awards that recognise innovation in Chile

Name of the Award	Dates	Managed by	Purpose
Concurso Funciona[6]	Since 2013 (ongoing)	*Dirección Nacional del SC*	Recognition of analytical skills, creativity, innovation and management improvements developed and implemented by civil servants
Concurso Chile Gestiona[7]	2013	*Ministerio de Hacienda*	To recognise the capacity for innovation, creativity and improved management of the processes developed in public services.

Source: *Laboratorio de Gobierno*

Funciona! recognises teams of civil servants who have created innovative initiatives in their institutions, with an effect on internal efficiency and/or in the quality of services provided to citizens. The three winning teams undertake an international internship which aims at giving them innovative experience in their professional areas. To raise awareness about this contest, the DNSC has created the role of institutional co-ordinators for *Funciona!*, whose main tasks involve encouraging the participation of officials, developing internal processes to select initiatives, and reviewing applications for compliance with the requirements. The rise in the number of co-ordinators (99 in 2014, 129 in 2015 and 150 in 2016) and in the number of applications to *Funciona!* suggests an increase in the interest and motivation to work towards more public sector innovation, and a potentially positive impact of the competition on PSI.

Applications to *Funciona!* are assessed according to five criteria: innovation (30%), results (30%), replicability (20%), user participation (10%), gender (5%) and formal aspects (5%). The replicability criteria is particularly important to contribute to sustainable public sector innovation. An award should be more than recognition of the accomplishment of a process; it should encourage future innovations and innovators by raising awareness on PSI, building capacity and being replicable in other institutions. For example, data from Denmark's Innovation Barometer which surveyed 1 255 public institutions in Denmark suggests that as much as 60%[8] of public innovations in Denmark are inspired by other people's solutions, and 13% are copied from others. Awards such as *Funciona!* are ideal tools to support this kind of replication.

Nevertheless, data suggests that in most cases public innovation awards are not fully used to their potential. The far most common usage of award winning innovations is to give credit to innovators by sharing the innovations publicly, and the replication of innovations is surprisingly very low (see Figure 3.1).

Figure 3.1. How are award-winning innovations used in OECD countries? (2016)

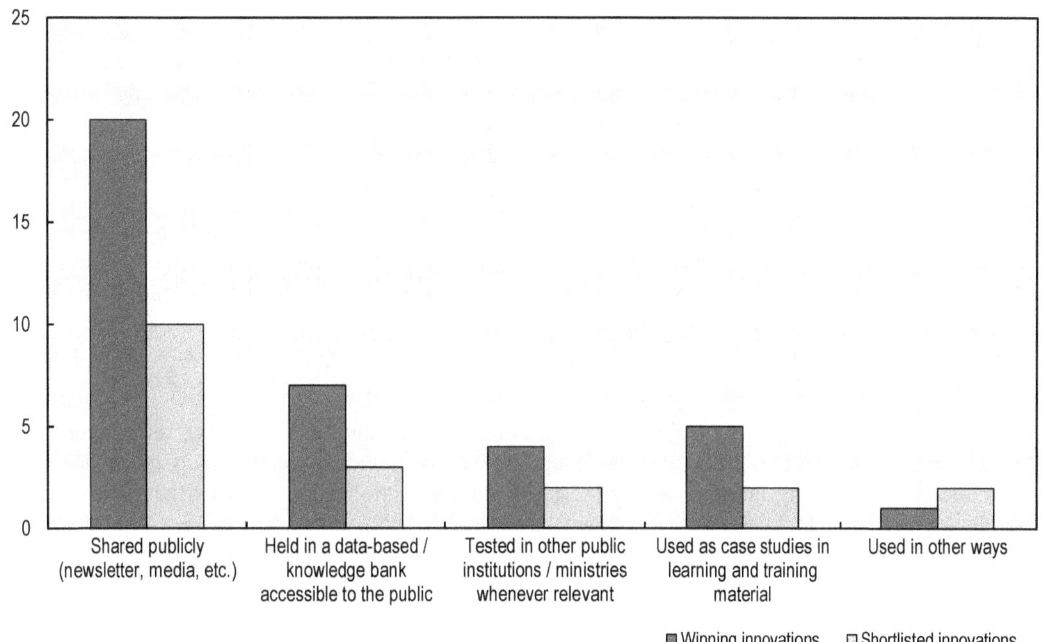

Source: 2016 Survey on Strategic Human Resource Management in Central/Federal Governments of OECD Countries.

One of the reasons that could explain the low level of the replication of innovations could be the asymmetry of skills between different public institutions, and the mobility schemes suggested in chapter 1 could help fill some of the skills and experience gaps. But another reason could also be related to low communication between institutions, or different levels of understanding of public sector innovation.

To fully exploit the potential impact of the *Functiona!* it should exist within a broader innovation ecosystem as a tool to reward, inspire and replicate. The South African example in Box 3.5 below is a good example, as the award is not something that signals the end of the innovation, but is a strategic enabler to expand the impact of that innovation. It uses winners and shortlisted innovations for teaching and inspiration, but also for replication. In Chile, the replication of innovations could be further encouraged through the implementation of incentives that could be integrated into future editions of innovation contests such as *Funciona!*. For example, although the award of *Funciona!* is certainly motivating, from the perspective of the sustainability of PSI, greater attention could be paid to the follow-up of the study trip. This could include an analysis of replicability of international practices, presentation of the findings to other Chilean administrations, or elaboration of a case study to be used in trainings.

Box 3.5. South Africa's Public Sector Innovation Awards: a focus on replication

In South Africa, the Annual Public Sector Innovation Awards have taken place every year since 2003, ensuring that public sector innovators are identified, recognised and appropriately rewarded. The programme is run by the CPSI, a Government Component reporting to the Minister for Public Service and Administration. The mandate of the CPSI is to entrench the culture and practice of innovation in the South African Public Sector.

The awards programme fits into a broader initiative to create and sustain an enabling environment for innovation in the public sector. The rationale behind the Awards is multifold: to give recognition to and celebrate the successes of innovators who are already leading the way to more effective, efficient and accountable government, to encourage the sharing of innovative practices to avoid re-inventing the wheel and to entrench creativity and excellence in the public sector.

One of the challenges with Awards programmes is that they are perceived as a ceremony rather than a programme. The CPSI has therefore strengthened the value-chain to ensure that shortlisted and winning innovations are assessed for replication potential, as often innovations tended to remain locked in "pockets of excellence" with little scaling up. The Awards programme therefore serves as a feeder-programme for the CPSI's replication programme. At least two of the innovations are selected annually, based on the potential for replication, but from 2017 onwards this will grow to between 5-10 projects (depending on the level of complexity). Their replication to other provinces or in other sectors is therefore facilitated in the following year. The CPSI is currently establishing a project management unit dedicated to supporting replication/scaling initiatives. As such, the Awards ceremony is but one element of an integrated approach.

Source: Center for Public Service Innovation, http://www.cpsi.co.za/.

Challenges to source innovative ideas and mobilise actors

The *Laboratorio de Gobierno* is using another kind of strategy focused on sourcing innovation from within and outside the public sector, creating learning opportunities, and accompanying public employees in the transformation of their own ideas into innovations. Impacta Salud and Aulab, both launched in 2015 after the *Laboratorio* was set up, were an initial milestone in this sense. Both challenges aimed at collecting ideas from the users' perspective (civil society, entrepreneurs and post-secondary educational institutions) to develop solutions that respond to user's needs and, as such, are a real source of public value.

Challenges like Impacta Salud and Aulab combine a monetary award with a grant to develop solutions (Box 3.6). As these programmes are very recent, their results are not yet fully understood. But similar initiatives in other countries have been proven successful so far, as for example the United States' Challenge.gov programme. Launched in 2010, this programme allowed citizens to participate in over 640 competitions launched by different agencies across the US federal government in technical, scientific, ideation, and creative areas where the US government seeks innovative solutions from the public.[9]

Box 3.6. Aulab and Impacta Salud

AULAB is an innovation platform launched in 2015 by the *Laboratorio de Gobierno*, which aims at making innovation policy democratic by increasing its outreach among actors from higher education institutions.

AULAB follows four main objectives:

- integrate innovative and transformative solutions from academia to the public sector
- mobilise students, academics and administrators across disciplines to collaboratively generate solutions to address national societal challenges
- constantly invigorate the public policy fabric by introducing new talents and ideas within the State
- converting academic research towards issues and challenges of high relevance and priority for citizens.

To date, two editions of AULAB open innovation challenges have taken place: AULAB Natural disasters was first launched in 2015 in co-operation with the Ministry of the Interior and the National Emergency Office (ONEMI), followed by AULAB Turismo in 2016 in co-operation with the Chilean Ministry of Economy, Development and Tourism.

Impacta is the public innovation challenges programme of the Government of Chile, implemented by the Laboratorio de Gobierno. Through Impacta, the Government calls for all the talents outside the State to be involved in public challenges, with new ideas, technologies, products or services.

To that purpose, Impacta:

- opens the State to the private talent through public challenges
- fosters a diverse ecosystem of Chilean and foreign entrepreneurs with innovative ideas
- incubates solutions, transforming them into viable prototypes with validated business models
- transforms the solutions into public policies that best meet citizen needs.

Impacta's first edition, *Impacta Salud*, was launched in 2015 in co-operation with the Ministry of Public Health and the municipality of Recoleta. Impacta Energy followed in 2016, in co-operation with the Ministry of Energy.

Source: *Laboratorio de Gobierno.*

The following table presents the particular purposes of each of the programmes:

Table 3.2. Selected innovation challenges in Chile aiming at finding sources of ideas for innovation

Name of the Award	Dates	Managed by	Purpose
Impacta Salud	Since 2015 (completed)	*Laboratorio de Gobierno*	Public innovation challenge targeting entrepreneurs to bring healthcare closer to user's needs so as to relieve overcrowding in family health centres and promote disease prevention and self-care.
Impacta Energia	Since 2016 (completed)	*Laboratorio de Gobierno*	Public Innovation challenge targeting entrepreneurs aiming at finding sources of ideas to promote access to energy, energy savings and energy as a source of development for Chileé
Aulab Onemi	2015 (completed)	*Laboratorio de Gobierno*	Through an open innovation challenge, AULAB Onemi sought to bring solutions from Higher Education Institutes to improve the effectiveness of reaction to natural disasters with regards to emergency housing, data management and volunteering mobilisation.
Aulab Turismo	2016 (completed)	*Laboratorio de Gobierno*	Bridge the gap between Higher Education Institutions and policy makers to co-create solutions to country challenges in the area of tourism, in line with the National Tourism Agenda.

Source: *Laboratorio de Gobierno.*

Now that Impacta and Aulab are into their second year, it is clear that the *Laboratorio* is integrating a learning-by-doing approach into its own programming as changes are made with a view to eventually perfecting the programmes. Taking a civil service development lens to these programmes, one can ask whether the potential of these programmes to increase skills and capacity among civil servants is maximised. While this is not the stated purpose of the programmes, the eventual results need to be owned by the public institution and therefor care should be taken to ensure their participation at every step.

Maximising the potential of the Public Innovators Community

Networks can support and motivate public sector innovation by creating a space where innovators can share ideas, practices and challenges for implementing innovations (see Figure 3.2). Innovators challenge the status quo and, consequently, they may often feel isolated within their own institutions. Networks put them in contact with other public employees facing similar challenges and as such networks can strengthen innovators' motivation to pursue their efforts.

Most OECD countries (22) have innovators' networks, such as Portugal's Common Knowledge Network RCC which is collaborative platform to promote the sharing of best practices and information about modernisation, innovation, and simplification of public administration. While the most common purpose of innovators' networks in OECD countries is to help members share their experience, the networks are quite frequently used to build the capacities of their members through training similarly to Flanders' Learning network on innovation in government; by providing support to develop specific projects; or by providing advice and guidance to public institutions as does Finland's Change Makers (Box 3.7).

Figure 3.2. Role of Innovator's Networks in building capacity for innovation (OECD countries, 2016)

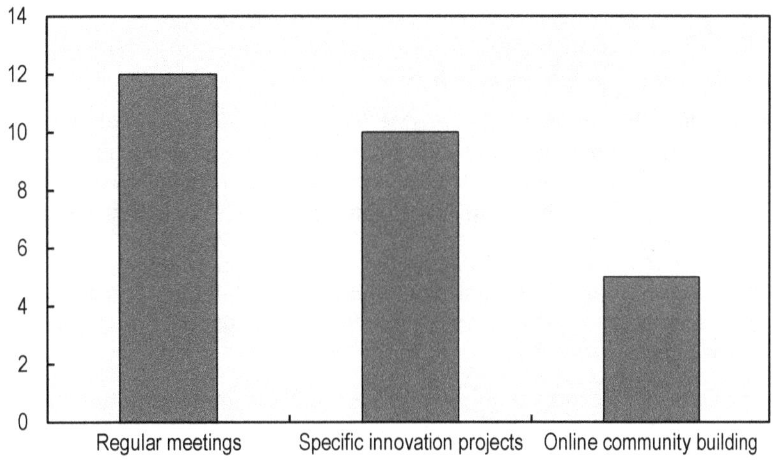

Source: 2016 Survey on Strategic Human Resource Management in Central/Federal Governments of OECD Countries.

While some networks are open to all people interested such as Italy's Innovatori PA, others aim at a specific population. Other countries like Denmark have "sub-networks" that target different audiences within the same network (Box 3.7).

Box 3.7. Public Innovators' networks

Italy: Innovatori PA

Innovatori PA is a social network of public employees and public sector consultants engaged in innovation. Through the online platform, innovators can create content and spaces for collaborative work, form working groups around topics of interest, open spaces for discussion and share projects and innovative experiences.

Finland: Change makers network

The Change Makers Network is a loosely organised and self-managed team of experts from different ministries, with different backgrounds, education and expertise. What is shared among the participants is the need and the will to build up a working culture based on a "whole government" - mindset and "crossing the silos" – ways of working.

The network is also willing to test and adopt modern, explorative and digital ways of working. Participants are all volunteers, and not appointed to represent any particular point of view or ministry in the network. The network model differs dramatically from the tradition where a working group or committee is set up and participants are appointed to fulfil a particular target, often determined elsewhere.

Change Makers Network is a new kind of a bottom-up community or "movement," which crosses boundaries of all kinds: administrative, professional, attitudinal, etc. It also strongly challenges traditional, hierarchical management practices as well as old-fashioned human resource management practices. Management practices as well as administrative services should all be seen as enabling renewal, instead of setting obstacles for change.

Change Makers Network´s unofficial mission statement is "Finland first". Only after that comes the sectoral approach. Through this mission statement, the network strongly stresses the need and the will to work across ministerial boundaries and silos in order enable problems in Finnish society to be solved.

Box 3.7. Public Innovators' networks *(continued)*

Portugal: Common Knowledge Network RCC

Launched in 2008, the Common Knowledge Network RCC is a collaborative platform to promote the sharing of best practices and information about the modernisation, innovation, and simplification of public administration. It is a network of knowledge sharing based on open membership by public bodies, central and local administrations, private entities and any citizen who wishes to participate.

The participation consists in presenting and describing a best practice and its results. The network thus seeks to assert itself as a reference device to support the dissemination of good practices and knowledge construction.

The RCC provides for debate on public policies and their implementation at local, regional and national levels, and participatory decision making with interest groups or communities of practice. It strengthens the relationships between the various stakeholders and co-ordinates information sharing.

It's an instrument that helps provide a common perspective on the activities of public administration to help standardise services and set up similar quality standards in different services.

Poland: Public Institutions Management Academy

At central level, Public Sector Innovation networks have a form of practitioners' meetings organised by the Chancellery of the Prime Minister as well as by the Lech Kaczyński National School of Public Administration, also within so-called Public Institutions Management Academy – a joint initiative of the School, the Social Insurance Institution, the Mazovian Voivodeship Office and THINKTANK - Centre for Dialogue and Analysis (social enterprise).

At the workshops in this Academy, its participants have an opportunity of having in-depth discussions regarding a selected field of public management (e.g. e-services, public participation in governance, competency model, performance appraisal, internal communication, cybersecurity). Additionally, a moderated panel discussion with the participation of external experts is part of such an event. Generally, some 80-100 officials attend the plenary session (panel discussion), followed by the workshops in groups of 15-30 persons. As regards the representation level, these meetings are basically open to experts irrespective of their seniority. The Academy also organises contests for public sector best practices in a given field. In 2016 the theme was innovative public services that meet the needs of the citizens.

Sources: Italy: Innovatori PA, www.innovatoripa.it; Finland: OECD Observatory of Public Sector Innovation (2015a), Change Makers Network, http://www.oecd.org/governance/observatory-public-sector-innovation/innovations/page/changemakersnetwork.htm; Portugal: OECD Observatory of Public Sector Innovation (2014), Common Knowledge Network RCC, http://www.oecd.org/governance/observatory-public-sector-innovation/innovations/page/commonknowledgenetworkrcc.htm; Poland: information provided by the PEM delegate.

Although institutional support for innovator's networks comes from the central public administration in most OECD countries, it's equally important to highlight that informal and self-driven PSI networks are the most common form of networks in OECD countries. These data suggest that civil servants are powerful driving forces for innovation, and building networks appears as a natural way of organisation that helps innovators support each other and eventually maximise the potential of their innovations across the public sector.

Chile started creating its first innovation network in 2015 (Box 3.8). Similarly to Austria, Denmark and the United States, the Chilean Public Innovators Network is placed under the central innovation institution, the *Laboratorio de Gobierno*, and it responds to the immediate need of giving some consistency to a myriad of smaller networks that were created informally by participants and award-winners of innovation contests throughout the years. GIP, *Funciona* and *Experimenta* winners are just some of the people that can support the consolidation and future development of the network. The Public Innovators Community has the potential to create a coherent group of public sector innovators, with a purpose that goes far beyond winning a particular award or contest.

In this regard, the Public Innovators Community is also part of the administration-wide effort to spread innovation across the public sector. While recognising innovators publicly and giving more visibility to innovations is a first step in this direction, the network also has the potential to create a new dynamics in public sector innovation.

Box 3.8. Chilean Network of Public Innovators

Launched in 2015, the Network of Public Innovators aims at being a movement of diverse actors motivated by the search for tools, experiences and approaches that facilitate the development of innovations to improve public services for their users. The network already counts 800 members from 15 regions. Of these, 156 have actively participated in activities. The network employs a threefold strategy:

1. **Collective Learning**: facilitate learning spaces between peers, where knowledge, approaches and methodologies could be shared, as well as good public innovation practices, to facilitate the development of new processes and initiatives. Activities to support this include a series of workshops on innovation tools and methodologies and regional meetings to highlight innovation practices in regional institutions and foster opportunities to implement practices and processes.
2. **Making public innovation visible**: make the experiences of public innovation of Chilean public servants more visible, communicating and disseminating initiatives of the actors of the Network so this can motivate others to innovate. Activities to support this include annual National Public Innovators Summits, meeting to get to know public innovators, and case collection/systematisation.
3. **Connecting motivations to innovate**: organise networking activities among the different members of the Network, through meetings and workshops to promote collaboration and increase social capital. Activities to support this include thematic meetings on a wide range of topics, including healthcare, public procurement, education, and public security.

Source: *Laboratorio de Gobierno.*

These new dynamics should depend of the capacity of the network to strengthen its members, but also on its interactions with other networks and the public sector as a whole. Internally, and possibly under the guidance of the Lab, the network should develop an action plan where learning spaces are a central component, in order to strengthen the capacity of its members as public sector innovators but also advocates for public sector innovation in their institutions. Externally, the network should engage with other networks, in order to disseminate information about innovation to other public sector target groups who may be less familiar with it, for example the future "Red ADP" for Senior Civil Servants.

A dynamic and successful network requires times and resources, and at least in this initial stage the Public Innovators Community will need some level of management and institutional support. The responsibility of launching and managing the Network is currently with the *Laboratorio de Gobierno* and the *NDSC* but, as the network evolves, there will be tension between enabling management of the network while at the same time allowing ownership among its members. The goal would be to push the Network to become more self-driven with time, while maintaining appropriate support and resources. This could be done by creating leadership roles for members and spaces for member-led initiatives, such as informal mentoring schemes.

Indeed, the success of the Network should partly depend on the capacity of the *Laboratorio de Gobierno* to anticipate the challenges and needs of a very diverse population of innovators, coming from a wide variety of areas. The organisation of activities is also likely to raise additional interest in public sector innovation and in the number of civil servants or institutions looking for support to develop innovations. While it is necessary to make the best use of the increase in visibility of the *Laboratorio* and of PSI, expectations and effective capacity to support the development of new innovations should be carefully balanced.

Conclusion and recommendations

On measuring and improving the organisational culture for more innovation

- Appropriate motivation triggers the use of skills for public sector innovation. As the organisational culture influences the perception of civil servants to move forward with innovative ideas, some tools can facilitate the creation of a more innovation-friendly organisational culture. In Chile, the organisational culture is often perceived as not supporting innovation. In this regard, the first thing needed to help better understand the influence of the organisational culture in the motivation of civil servants to innovate could be to measure it better. To this purpose, the *DNSC* could develop a survey module with questions about the perception of civil servants on their ability and motivation to innovate in their work, and also about the opportunities they have to implement their ideas.

On scaling up the potential of innovation awards

- Although Chile has developed a number of innovation contests and awards since the 1990's, there is space to scale up the impact of shortlisted and award-winning innovations. For example, greater attention could be put on making a larger set of innovations more publicly visible, for example, through an online platform like the OECD's OPSI; or by publicly recognising institutions that implemented innovative practices directly inspired by the award-winning or shortlisted innovations; or by developing programmes to replicate successful innovations.

On strengthening the network of innovators

- In addition, strengthening the network of innovators is also an important tool to recognise and support the innovators and to motivate other civil servants. The *Laboratorio* could support the Public Innovators Network with an action plan emphasising learning activities, for example national events (like the launching the network in November 2015) or smaller workshops, and use them to develop specific skills and provide information on PSI. The network could be used to promote the implementation of innovations directly inspired by examples from the Chilean public administration. This could be supported by the implementation of a mentoring scheme bringing together innovators and future innovators and managers of innovative teams/teams who wish to innovate. The development of the Public Innovators Community also raises questions about the present and future role of the *Laboratorio* as network manager to balance the need for network management with the need for members' ownership.

Notes

1 http://www.industry.gov.au/innovation/publicsectorinnovation/Documents/_APS_Innovation_Action_Plan.pdf

2 www.fedview.opm.gov/2016FILES/2016_FEVS_Gwide_Final_Report.PDF.

3 www.whitehouse.gov/sites/default/files/omb/memoranda/2015/m-15-04.pdf.

4 www.oecd.org/governance/observatory-public-sector-innovation/innovations/page/commitmenttoculturechange.htm.

5 www.per.gov.ie/en/customer-charter-initiative/.

6 Ex Desafío Chile Gestiona in 2012 and Desafío Innovación in 2013 and 2014.

7 Ex Premio a la innovacion en los servicios públicos (2012).

8 http://innovationsbarometer.coi.dk/main-results-in-english/.

9 http://www.challenge.gov/about

References

Amabile, Teresa M (1997), "Motivating Creativity in Organisations: On Doing what you Love and Loving what you Do", *California Management Review,* Fall 1997, 40, 1.

Boxall, Peter and John Purcess (2011), *Strategy and Human Resource Management,* Third Edition. Palgrave Mcmillan.

Center for Public Service Innovation, http://www.cpsi.co.za/.

Direccion Nacional del Servicio Civil (2013), Barómetro de la Gestión de Personas 2013, Resultados generales de la primera aplicación a servicios públicos y Modelo de Gestión de Personas 2013.

Feb web le portail du personnel fédéral Belgique (2011), Concours Innovation, véhicule d'efficience,www.fedweb.belgium.be/sites/default/files/downloads/20110905_reglement_concours_innovation.pdf

Fernandez, Sergio and Tima Moldogaziev (2012), "Using Employee Empowerment to Encourage Innovative Behavior in the Public Sector", *Journal of Public Administration Research and Theory Advance Access,* published May 23, 2012.

Foss, N. et al. (2009), "Encouraging Knowledge Sharing among Employees: How Job Design Matters", in *Human Resource Management*, November–December 2009, Vol. 48, No. 6, Pp. 871– 893.

Gee, S. and I. Miles (2008), Mini Study 04 – Innovation Culture, Global Review of Innovation Intelligence and Policy Studies, Pro Inno Grips, available at http://grips.proinnoeurope.eu/knowledge_base/dl/392/orig_doc_file.

Government of Ireland (2015), Civil Service Employee Engagement Survey, www.per.gov.ie/en/civil-service-employee-engagement-survey/.

Government of the United Kingdom/Cabinet Office (2015), Civil Service People Survey 2015, www.gov.uk/government/uploads/system/uploads/attachment_data/file/477335/csps2015_benchmark_report.pdf and www.gov.uk/government/publications/civil-service-people-survey-2015-results

Innovatori PA, www.innovatoripa.it.

Institute of Public Administration Australia, "Public Sector Innovation Awards", www.act.ipaa.org.au/innovation-awards.

Mumford, Michael D. (2000), "Managing Creative People: Strategies and Tactics for Innovation", *Human Resource Management Review*, Volume 10, Number 3, 2000, pages 313± 351.

OECD (2017), *Fostering Innovation in the Public Sector*, OECD Publishing, Paris. http://dx.doi.org/10.1787/9789264270879-en.

OECD (2016), *Engaging Public Employees for a High-Performing Civil Service*, OECD Public Governance Reviews, OECD Publishing, Paris, http://dx.doi.org/10.1787/9789264267190-en.

OECD (2015a), Observatory of Public Sector Innovation, Change Makers Network, http://www.oecd.org/governance/observatory-public-sector-innovation/innovations/page/changemakersnetwork.htm.

OECD (2015b), *The Innovation Imperative in the Public Sector: Setting an Agenda for Action*, OECD Publishing, Paris, http://dx.doi.org/10.1787/9789264236561-en.

OECD (2014), Observatory of Public Sector Innovation, Common Knowledge Network RCC,http://www.oecd.org/governance/observatory-public-sector-innovation/innovations/page/commonknowledgenetworkrcc.htm

Orazi, D. C., Turrini A., Valotti G., (2013), "Public sector leadership: new perspectives for research and practice", in *International Review of Administrative Sciences*, 79(3) 486–504.

Partnership for Public Service, The Best Places to Work in the Federal Government, http://bestplacestowork.org/BPTW/rankings/categories/large/innovation.

Chapter 4.

Opportunities for Chilean public employees to innovate

This chapter discusses the opportunities available for Chile's public employees to contribute to innovation in their organisations. Creating the right organisational environment for public sector innovation is core leadership and management responsibility. The chapter explores two factors that contribute to this responsibility. First, it discusses how creating a common vision for public sector innovation could help to build the innovation narrative in Chile, develop shared understanding of goals, and align action across the public sector. Second, the chapter looks at the role that public leaders and managers in the Chilean public sector play to implement that vision and create the space and opportunities for innovation in their organisations. This includes promoting innovative ways of working, and sustaining efforts to embed innovative practices in the public sector.

A workforce of highly capable (Chapter 2) and motivated (Chapter 3) public sector innovators will only achieve real innovation if they are provided with opportunities to put those skills and motivation to use. Innovation requires a level of autonomy – employees need to feel a level of freedom, trust and ownership in the way they approach and resolve problems creatively. This requires clear roles, goals and expectations to structure autonomy in a way that ensures it aligns with results. This also requires trust-based leadership and management. Innovation will not happen through regulation. Leaders and managers need to trust in the capacity of their employees to handle delegation, take decisions and work in partnerships. Finally, creating opportunities for employees to innovate also means creating safe spaces to test ideas and experiment through trial and error to learn and improve.

This chapter looks at how civil servants in Chile are provided with the opportunity to put abilities and motivation into use to achieve impact. It assesses the policies, programmes and institutions that help create space for innovation, and discusses the role of leadership in ensuring that capable and motivated civil servants are provided with the chance to innovate.

The chapter explores two main factors that contribute to providing opportunities for Chilean civil servants to innovate. First, it discusses how creating a common vision for public sector innovation could help to build the innovation narrative in Chile, develop shared understanding of goals implied, and align action across the public sector. Second, and relatedly, the chapter looks at the role that public leaders and managers in the Chilean public sector play to implement that vision and create the space and opportunities for innovation in their organisations. This includes promoting innovative ways of working, and in sustaining efforts and embedding innovative practices in the public sector.

Assessment of opportunities to innovate in Chile's public services

The Chilean public employees, managers and senior leaders who participated in interviews and workshops conducted as part of this review spoke quite consistently of limited opportunities to put their innovation skills into practice. Many spoke of the need for more resources, time, training, management and leadership approaches to create spaces for innovation. There is a sense that rigid legal and budgetary structures limit opportunities for innovation. Some went as far as to state that the goal of building an innovative state is to address the rigidities of the state. Public innovators pointed to the Lab as an essential partner in this area, but the size and breadth of the challenge is too great for one lab to take on alone.

Many of the innovators and leaders who contributed to this research painted a picture of isolated incidents of innovation and small islands of good practice, but with no framework and connecting tissue to bring it together as a whole. Many informants expressed a view that not all public leaders or managers have a common understanding of what innovation means in the context of Chile's public sector. While public sector innovation is mentioned in the current Government's programme, there is no articulated strategic vision that can guide leaders and managers on how to use innovation to transform government policies and services in their ministries and agencies.

Discussions with senior leaders in the Chilean public sector highlighted a central role for organisational leadership to provide opportunities for citizen and employee-driven innovation. Organisational leaders' core job is to align the mandate and strategic objectives of their organisation to its management processes so that tasks are accomplished as effectively as possible. Leaders then have ample opportunities to align these systems in ways that provide opportunities for their employees to innovate. The discussions with leaders highlighted a number of ways that some of Chile's senior leaders have created opportunities for successful innovation in their organisations:

- **Give permission to civil servants to innovate in their organization**. Leaders highlighted that their role in creating opportunities for civil servants to innovate was to give a mandate for innovation within their organisation.
- **Remove the psychological barriers and self-perceived constraints for innovation**. When legal frameworks are complex and unclear, civil servants have a tendency to interpret them conservatively so as not to end up on the wrong side of the law. This, combined with a "we've always done it this way" culture, can have the effect of limiting the perception of opportunities for innovation even when the law allows it. Leaders can help clarify the legal framework underlying innovation and ensure civil servants have the ability to fully balance compliance with existing rules and use of discretionary authority.
- **Communicate the value, benefits and clear results of innovation**. Leaders highlighted the need to display the results of innovation projects, reward innovators and champion success cases. Leaders must be able to show and communicate the added value of innovative projects. This suggests the need to invest also in impact measurement.
- **Build a trust relationship with managers and their teams**. It was noted that senior leaders need to trust middle managers and their teams, and provide them with the autonomy, space and mandate necessary for innovation.
- **Create the conditions for innovation, and then get out of the way**. Senior leaders recognise that their role is to generate the conditions for middle managers to create space (and time) for their teams to innovate, but for them to stay away from the direct innovation process. Senior leaders also noted that innovative ideas often come from the bottom up and the frontlines of service delivery. In this case, they highlighted their role as being in a position to steer their organisation in such a way that provides opportunities for those ideas to be brought forward and encouraged, which includes bringing about a wider culture change in favour of innovation.

Much of the discussion with senior leaders focused on leadership within their organisations. There was little discussion, however, of the leaders' roles in forging the kinds of institutional partnerships required to enable innovation across and between sectors. Nor was there much discussion on how to provide opportunities for civil servants to engage with users and the broader citizenship. This reinforces the sense that, so far, innovation is framed as a closed system in Chile's public administration.

This review also provided an opportunity to identify skills used by middle managers to support public sector innovation in the organisations in which they work. The managers who participated in the interviews and workshops conducted by the OECD and the *Laboratorio* identified some of the skills that they had used during the different phases of the innovative processes in their institutions. While they use many of the same skills as innovators, such as the capacity to understand the users' needs (Figure 1.3 Chapter 1), managers often emphasised that having the capacity to analyse a problem and the capacity to motivate and to engage the whole team were key elements for transforming an idea into an innovation.

In the implementation phase of an innovation, managers also emphasised the need to have the capacity to co-ordinate teams and communicate effectively so to obtain support from the political level or even from users or other stakeholders, as well as resilience and perseverance to keep the team motivated in face of resistance. Communication and negotiation skills remain important in all innovation phases; to increase the impact of an innovation some of the most important skills were the capacity to make information systematic, look for additional resources, and anticipate proactively.

Despite the impressive level of ability and commitment displayed by the middle managers who participated in the review, many of the participants, from innovators to leaders, seemed to feel that most middle managers in the Chilean public administration do not fit this mould. Many interviewees suggested that the innovation commitment was high at senior levels and at the lowest, but that there was a blockage somewhere in the middle. This issue is a fact that has affected many of the processes carried out by innovators that were consulted, especially those who were part of the GIP initiatives. This may be due to substantial workloads and stress, as well as to performance systems which reward narrow definitions of successful delivery. Part of the problem is also likely institutional: while SADP is managed collectively, the middle managers are not. Therefor little training or development is directed at them. Many middle managers may have been promoted due to excellent performance in their previous positions, with little support for the transition to their new managerial roles.

Creating and sustaining a vision for public sector innovation

Chile's trajectory of public administration reform and modernisation has been impressive and it is a true leader in Latin America. The introduction of the report highlights many successes achieved related to public sector modernisation and digital government. Even though President Bachelet's invitation to achieve an innovative builds on these successes, it also represents a change in vision, to a more participatory approach building on the input of citizens and civil servants and redefining the relationship between state and citizen. This has profound implications for the way public leaders should run their public services.

Building this vision participatively, and codifying it in an official statement of some form, could help to align public leadership and action around public sector innovation objectives across the Chilean public sector.

The concept of a public sector innovation policy agenda is recent and not widespread in OECD countries. To date, there are relatively few countries to have set up a dedicated agenda or blueprint to support public sector innovation. Traditionally, initiatives to foster innovation in the public sector have been associated as part of technology or change management policies at both central and sectoral level, or framed as a small but significant part of larger vision for innovation in the economy. Only recently, countries have started to include innovation as part of their civil service enhancement agendas and/or building a distinct agenda for innovation.

Experience from OECD countries indicates that a public sector innovation policy can be instrumental in setting up and articulating a vision for the use of innovation in the public sector; helping to identify common goals and prioritising action across the public sector; motivating the public sector to work jointly and lowering resistance to change by engaging civil servants and developing common narratives. The examples of Canada and Australia could provide Chile with useful insights into approaches for the development of a comprehensive vision for public sector innovation in government.

The Canadian federal government has developed the Blueprint 2020 vision for a world-class public service, which embodies innovation in many of its transformation and modernisation elements, and which civil servants built from the ground up. Public employees were engaged in a discussion around the vision and in the development of an action plan. This engagement process was largely bottom up, with public servants offering opinions, ideas, and innovative solutions. At the same time, implementation of the horizontal initiative is led by the Clerk of the Privy Council, who provides overall horizontal leadership to a board of management and public service renewal, which ensures that the strategy is followed through down to departmental level. The government of Canada found this approach helpful in starting a broader discussion among civil servants about how they saw their role in contributing to innovation, but also in engaging them in identifying and launching their own change agendas. At the same time, there was leadership for the initiative, and it was supported at the highest levels of government, including by the Prime Minister.

In 2015, the Australian federal government established a service-wide innovation agenda in the Australian Public Service, and which is endorsed by departmental secretaries (part of the senior executive service in Australia) and sets commitments from top management for supporting the agenda. Two main priorities were set for implementation over a one year time period, including agreeing to better connect civil servants to share ideas and experiences about doing things differently, and promote initiatives that give opportunities for the public service to share, develop, test, grow and recognise good ideas. While these priorities and accompanying actions were informed by experience of public servants from the innovators network, the agenda was largely set and commutated from the top down. Though still in its early stages after only a year, the change in language and a common narrative coming from senior leaders about the value of public sector innovation has been seen to be helpful in the Australian context.

While setting the right agenda and motivating civil servants will probably require a combination of top-down and bottom-up initiatives, there are some interesting lessons that could be taken from these experiences when looking at the specific Chilean context. Support from top decision makers (Canada), combined with possibilities for bottom-up involvement could work well to ensure leadership commitment during the process and motivate civil servants to see themselves as active contributors. Engaging Chilean public employees in a common dialogue about the civil service's role in contributing to innovation could be a first step. Engaging top levels in such a discussion could also be a way of showing the value and the benefits of innovating in the public sector, and as a way to raise awareness in leaders of public sector organisations who might be less familiar with the public sector innovation mandate.

In Chile there is no public sector innovation agenda bringing together and articulating a shared vision for public sector innovation in central government. Nor is there a formal mechanism to ensure experiences and lessons emerging from implementation are shared. The Board of the *Laboratorio* stands out as the only formal co-ordination mechanism but its action is limited to providing supervision and direction for the Lab initiatives.

Senior leaders creating the space for innovation

Top leaders steer organisations, set goals, align resources, and play a significant role in the development of organisational culture and climate (Chapter 2). Leaders have the power and influence to structure organisations, select skilled employees, open doors and remove barriers for the people, projects and teams they support. Without the support and commitment of top leadership, public sector innovation cannot take hold.

However public sector innovation is not a top-down process and herein lies the interesting challenge. While top leaders need to be key players to create a supportive organisational environment for innovation, they also need to have confidence in the abilities of their managers and civil servants, to provide them with the autonomy required for bottom-up innovation to take place. As one participant in the OECD workshops put it, "create the conditions and get out of the way". In this sense, leadership for innovation suggests the need to delegate leadership to all levels of an organisation, to enable and inspire leadership behaviours at even the lowest levels of an organisational hierarchy.

This section looks at the role of senior leaders and middle managers in the Chilean public sector, to create space and opportunities for innovation in their organisations and teams. It presents some of the key findings from interviews with leaders and managers during the OECD's fact-finding mission in November 2015 and from the roundtable organised with Chilean public sector leaders during the second mission in March 2016.

Innovation as a competency in Chile's Senior Executive Service programme

Senior leaders in this section refer to the Senior Executive Service (SADP – *Sistema de Alta Direccion Publica*) mentioned in the introduction, composed of the first and second levels of public organisations' management hierarchies, and overseen by the DNSC. Unlike most civil servants, senior leaders are hired through a specific recruitment system which includes a competency framework against which candidates are assessed. This programme is the region's most successful merit-based selection and management system for senior public leaders, which has helped to ensure highly qualified executives are selected to lead the modernisation of Chile's public sector and the overall economic and social development. The existence of a centralised, merit-based programme for selecting and managing senior executives places Chile among a growing group of OECD countries who increasingly recognise the value of ensuring merit at the highest levels (Figure 4.1).

Figure 4.1. Use of separate HRM practices for Senior Civil Servants

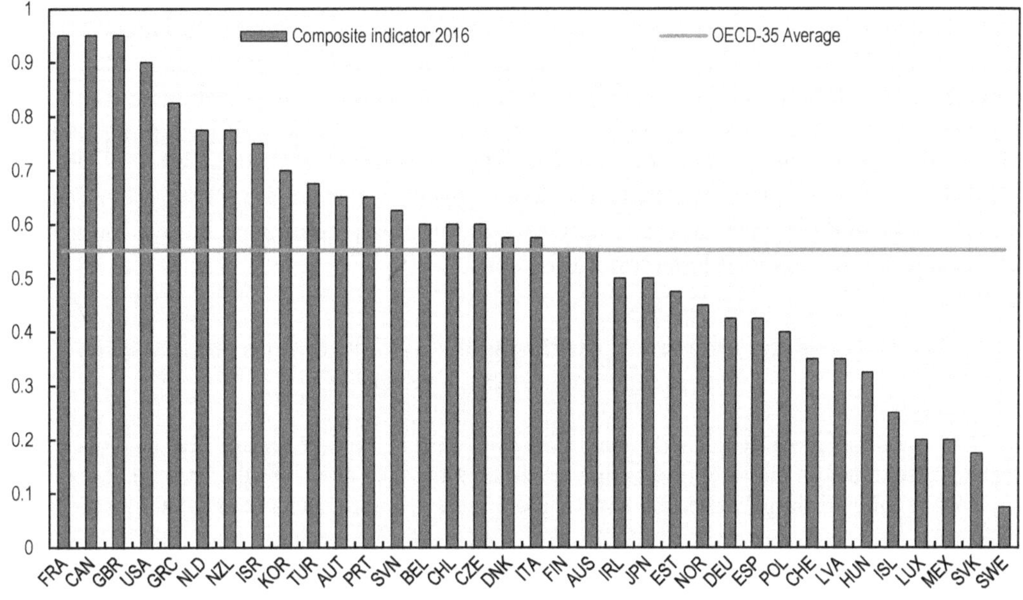

Source: 2016 Survey on Strategic Human Resource Management in Central/Federal Governments of OECD Countries.

Chile's SADP ensures that innovation-oriented skills and competencies are considered at the recruitment stage of senior leaders. By law, institutions include "Innovation and Flexibility" as one of the seven leadership competencies in all SADP job descriptions. This is defined in this context as the ability to transform barriers and complexities into opportunities; to incorporate new practices, procedures and methodologies into institutional plans; and to take calculated risks that allow the creation of solutions, promote change and improve results. In addition, senior leaders are expected to demonstrate competencies in strategic vision, internal leadership and people management, and external leadership and network building, among others.

Recruitment organisations assign weights to each competency and they are tested through competency-based interview methods and other psychological testing and reference checks. A first shortlist is submitted to the Selection committee, who conducts a final interview. The DNSC presents the three or four best candidates to the appointing authority, who can either select one of them or call for a new job advertisement.

Including innovation among the selection criteria of senior managers helps to reinforce this theme as a leadership value, however this should also be reinforced through ongoing development opportunities and performance assessment. How the competency "innovation and flexibility" is demonstrated at selection and reinforced throughout the careers of SADP in Chile is unclear. Providing opportunities for senior leaders to reflect on their role as leaders of a more innovative civil service can be done through leadership development programmes, networks and performance management systems. But a first step would require looking for examples of the kinds of leadership behaviour that demonstrate this particular competency in action.

These findings highlight behaviours that are in line with those emerging from the experience of other countries. Australia, for example, has worked with its innovation champions group, a network of senior leaders committed to a more innovative public sector, to define the kinds of behaviours that leaders need to display to support innovation in their organisations (Box 4.1). Canada has undergone a similar activity, identifying the kinds of behaviours required at each level of the hierarchy to "promote innovation and guide change", one of its key leadership competencies. At the highest level, leaders are expected to champion a culture that challenges the status quo and encourages responsible risk taking, encourage experimentation and genuine evaluation of outcomes, among others. Following the Australian and Canadian examples to "unpack" the DNSC's competency on innovation and flexibility could provide a basis for further development of a senior leadership cadre in Chile with a common understanding of innovation and the actions needed to support it in their organisations.

Box 4.1. Leading innovation: exhibiting behaviours that create space and encourage civil servants to innovate

Innovation is about people – whether it's about getting support for an idea, having people actually use or act on the idea, or thinking about what the idea does for other people. Because it is about people, it is largely tied to interacting with others, and the behaviours that are modelled. If leaders want to encourage innovation then they need to exhibit behaviours that will lead to innovative thinking and doing on the part of their employees. Working with the Innovation Champions Group (a senior leaders group in the Australian Public Service - (Box 4.2)), the Australian government examined what behaviours leaders needed to be shown (or avoided) to support and encourage civil servants to innovate. The following is the 'beta' version of behaviours for leaders that has been developed, as endorsed by the Innovation Champions Group:

1. **Empower others – share where innovation is most needed.** Innovation often works best when it is a strategic activity. One of the easiest ways to empower others to innovate is to let them know where it is most needed or where it is most sought. This can help others focus on ideas that are more likely fit with strategic needs and aims.
2. **Invite in the outliers – demonstrate that diversity is valued.** Innovation involves new ways of looking at things, and that requires tapping into different networks and groups and experiences, different ways of working and thinking, and allowing and encouraging constructive debate. One way to foster an environment that values diversity is to actively invite in those with different perspectives, from outside and inside your organisation. Who are the outliers that represent new or different ways of understanding your world? Invite them into the conversation and show that you are open to very different insights.
3. **Say "Yes, and" not "No, because".** It can be hard to put forward a new idea, but very easy to stop someone else doing it. "A raised eyebrow or a sceptical look can kill an idea before it gets any oxygen". Building on an idea can help ensure you don't miss out on a great new way of doing things. It helps people know that you value ideas and creativity, and that ideas are not expected to be perfect straight away.
4. **Don't over-react – appreciate experimental error.** Things will go wrong. There will be mistakes as things are learnt through innovation. Some, if not most, ideas will fail to come to anything. People will try things that don't work. One adverse reaction to an innovative attempt can stop any further innovation. Provide guidance on where there is room to experiment, and where there can only be rigorously tested and checked initiatives. Create space for 'safe' experimentation. Cultivate reflective learning, where experimental mistakes are discussed and learnt from, and not hidden or seen as shameful.

Box 4.1. Leading innovation: exhibiting behaviours that create space and encourage civil servants to innovate *(continued)*

5. **Support innovators and share stories of success.** Innovation can be hard. It can be hard going against the status quo or working on something that may not, initially, fit with the rest of an organisation. Developing a new idea can involve running into a lot of roadblocks. Innovative ideas will require time and resources to be developed into real and tested proposals. They will need protection from the ongoing pressures of business-as-usual work. Innovators will need to be supported. Sharing stories of success can help build wider support, demonstrate the value that innovation can bring and show that it can be done, and help connect those who have implemented something new with those who are trying to do something new.

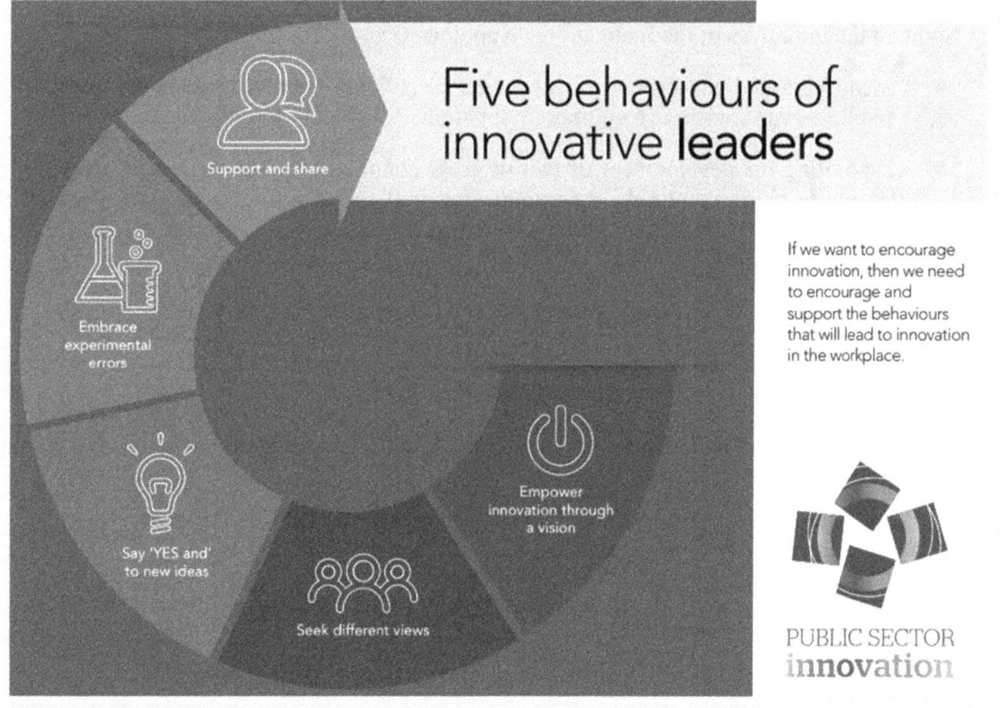

Source: Roberts, A. (15 February 2016), "Innovation Behaviours for the Public Service – beta version", Australian Government, Public Sector Innovation, http://innovation.govspace.gov.au/2016/02/15/innovation-behaviours-for-the-public-service-beta-version/.

A senior leader's network could provide a forum to debate and develop these behaviours, share practical experiences about creating space for innovation within organisations, and also to discuss shared innovation issues and challenges. It can also be used as a space to collaborate on demonstration projects that explore and typify new ways of working, and can contribute to cross-agency initiatives to encourage a culture of innovation. For example, the Innovation Champions Group in the Australian Public Service is of a group of senior leaders with representation from each department that meet regularly to learn from each other and are charged with championing innovation within their organisation (Box 4.2). This network is led by the Department of Industry, Innovation and Science, which is responsible for leading the innovation agenda across the government.

Box 4.2. Connecting Innovation and Strategic Leadership: The Innovation Champions Group of the Australian Public Service

How can senior leaders learn from each other about how to best support innovators and innovative activity in their agencies? How can whole-of-service ideas for new ways of doing best be explored and tested?

In July 2015 the Portfolio Secretaries of the Australian Public Service (APS) endorsed the creation of an 'Innovation Champions Group'. The group of senior leaders is chaired by the Department of Industry, Innovation and Science and has provided a forum to share practical experiences about supporting innovation within agencies, discussing shared innovation issues and challenges, collaborating on demonstration projects that explore and typify new ways of working, and contributing to cross-agency initiatives to foster a culture of innovation.

Some of the initiatives of the Innovation Champions Group have included:

- identifying and endorsing a set of model behaviours for both leaders and individual public servants wishing to support innovation
- supporting the development of two projects nominated by officer-level staff – one a design thinking mentoring programme for staff to share and learn from each other about design thinking; and one investigating how crowdsourcing can practically help inform policymaking
- supporting a trial cross-agency training project on complex problems for APS staff
- learning about new technologies and business models that might have an impact on the work of the public service, such as BlockChain
- supporting and participating in Innovation Month, including the inaugural Innovation Awards.

Sources: Beauchamp, Glenys (2015), "Innovation Month and Supporting Innovation Across the APS", Australian Government, Public Sector Innovation, http://innovation.govspace.gov.au/2015/07/06/innovation-month-and-supporting-innovation-across-the-aps/; Hazlehurst, D. (30 March 2016), "Sixth Meeting of the Innovation Champions Group", Australian Government, Public Sector Innovation, http://innovation.govspace.gov.au/2016/03/30/sixth-meeting-of-the-innovation-champions-group/.

Chile's innovation-oriented competencies for senior leaders can also be reinforced through the performance management system. In Canada for example, senior leaders are charged with promoting innovation though the performance management system. Key leadership competencies are used to assess public service executives in the context of performance assessment and promotion criteria. Promoting innovation and guiding change is one of the key leadership competencies for all federal executives, in recognition of the role that public service leaders play in creating an environment that supports bold thinking, experimentation and intelligent risk taking.

In Chile, the DNSC draws up guidelines to help institutions design performance criteria for senior civil servants (ADP). As the performance objectives must be coherent with the institutional strategy, planning and management systems, budget, existing PMGs, and team performance (*convenios de desempeño colectivo*), there is space to include more innovation-related objectives for senior managers. This is especially important given the window of opportunity presented by the new law which will bring a greater role to the DNSC for ongoing performance management of SADP leaders. For example, although performance criteria are not explicitly included in the guidelines[1] of the DNSC for the elaboration of *convenios de desempeño* for the senior civil servants, since innovation is one of the recruitment criteria it should be possible to include it in the performance evaluation of ADP.

A third way of reinforcing the innovation-oriented competencies of the ADP is through leadership development programmes focused both on innovation and good management in general. And here it is important to extend the focus of analysis beyond the highest level to include all managers of teams, projects and units.

Managing innovation: The role of middle managers making space in their teams for innovation

Innovative projects and teams require a different approach to management which move away from command-and-control models towards greater emphasis on working across boundaries, focusing on outcomes and creating space to test new ideas through iteration (OECD, 2015). Because innovation is by definition novel, there is no recipe to follow. Managing innovation requires project and team managers who demonstrate the ability to build diverse teams, trust these teams and, within a goal-oriented environment, give the autonomy to manage complex and ambiguous projects, manage risk, align resources in uncertain environments and adjust as they go. With the right set of skills, managers can inspire and motivate their teams to be innovative, and help scale up the work of public innovators by advocating for this work among senior management and other stakeholders.

In many cases the skills to manage innovation are the skills of all good public managers, which are particularly tested when involved in an innovation project. Such skills cannot be assumed to accrue naturally, especially in situations when managers are promoted due to good performance in professional positions or as subject matter experts. Good legal experts, for example, do not automatically make for good managers of a legal department. The skill set is specific, and priority needs to be given to development and recruitment/promotion criteria.

Skill sets such as those described in the assessment section of this chapter can be used to help develop recruitment criteria and training policies to attract, recruit and develop the kind of managers needed for successful public sector innovation. In Chile, middle managers are recruited through a procedure which is very similar to the one for all civil servants. In this framework, the *DNSC* only intervenes by advertising the position and supports Ministries upon request in the definition of selection criteria. As there is no competency model to serve as a basis for recruitment of middle managers, the inclusion of innovation-oriented skills and competencies is done at the discretion of the appointing authority – and, as such, the recruitment of middle managers is very similar to the recruitment of the all other public employees. In this regard, it is up to the leaders of each public institution in Chile to identify the kinds of innovation-oriented skills they look for in their public managers and highlight these in development, recruitment and promotion criteria. A middle management competency framework could help, although it is unclear who in Chile would have authority to develop such a framework and monitor its implementation.

Developing middle and senior managers' abilities to lead innovation

Recent research suggests that the abilities of middle managers to manage people effectively have a very significant impact on organisational performance. This is probably the case in Chile's civil service where senior leaders tend to stay in their positions for only two to three years on average. This may limit the ability to really develop their institution's innovation capacity, which requires a long-term sustained commitment. This situation suggests that any innovation-oriented management development strategy must take middle managers into account as they tend to stay longer in their positions.

Leadership and executive development is among the highest priorities for civil service reform in OECD countries today. According to a recent survey, 19 OECD countries report including public sector innovation as a key component of leadership development, however it is not yet the case in Chile. This means that Chile can benefit from additional experiences and build its development programme for public managers from internal and international best practices. In Israel for example, leadership for innovation is emphasised through the National College of Leadership, Governance and Management; Estonia and Finland (Box 4.3) have put together a training programme "Innovation BootCamp" for leaders of both countries, and Estonia also emphasises innovation in the central training and development programmes for mid-level managers; Norway includes innovation leadership and management in development programmes for top managers and management groups (OECD, 2016 SHRM). The Australia and New Zealand School of Government (ANZSOG) has also developed a programme on "Delivering Better Outcomes for Lower Costs: Leading public sector innovation"[2] to help senior public servants think and act innovatively about challenges within their department or agency. The training focuses on understanding the distinction between innovation and change or reform, creating a culture open to innovation within an organisation, creating systems and processes that robustly support innovation, devising innovative solutions to specific problems and developing action plans, and leading teams to effectively implement plans.

Box 4.3. Training senior and middle management in Estonia and Belgium

Estonia and Finland: Innovation Bootcamp

The Innovation Boot Camp was a one-year development programme for Senior Managers from Estonia and Finland, with the purpose to increase the strategic agility and innovation capacity of senior managers. The programme was structured into seven modules: innovator/leader, innovation culture, innovation tools in the global context, rapid change and implementation, foresight thinking, sustainability and vision/roadmap.

The programme was organised in different cities in Estonia, Finland, India, Austria and the USA. It consisted of site visits, conferences with speakers from the private and public sectors, dedicated development projects and coaching support.

Estonia: Development of mid-level managers: Enhancing leadership skills and promoting common values in the civil service

Middle managers are the key players in spreading common values in Estonia's decentralised civil service and implementing change. To enhance their leadership skills and promote common values across the civil service, the Estonian Ministry of Finance in 2012 launched horizontal development and coaching programmes for middle managers.

Box 4.3. Training senior and middle management in Estonia and Belgium *(continued)*

Both programmes are based on a competency framework of middle managers including five core competencies – area development, leadership, personal development, process management, communication and co-operation.

The comprehensive development programme for mid-level managers (KAJA) offers a unique combination of development support, practical exercises and training to ensure the fulfilment of the objectives set in the personal development programme of each participant. The programme aims at developing skills, knowledge and qualities that help middle level managers perform better in their position and strives to unify the understanding of the middle manager′s role by promoting transorganisational co-operation and creating communication networks. The group work carried out under the programme includes solving concrete policy-making problems jointly, helping to contribute to the reforms taking place in real time.

The coaching programme for middle managers offers participants an opportunity to learn from experienced managers, combined with a tailored approach to each individual participant. The main benefits of the programme are disseminating the coaching style in public sector management together with the solutions to real life management issues created with the co-operation of coaches and coachee.

Belgium: Vitruvius and In Vivo leadership development programmes

The Vitruvius and In Vivo leadership development programmes in Belgium aim at developing the leadership skills of managers and future managers throughout the federal government. Vitruvius is a leadership development programme for middle managers in federal government agencies. Each year, 60 strategic middle managers are accepted into the programme. In Vivo is an individual leadership programme for 100 top managers yearly.

The objective of the programmes is to improve the capacity of public organisations by developing strategic key managers who will contribute to establishing the desired culture of result-oriented leadership. Each organisation nominates key managers for each programme.

An inductive learning approach is an integral part of these programmes, where self-reflection is encouraged. Each participant is supported by a methodological portfolio and "peer coaching" to facilitate the transfer of learning in everyday life.

Belgium: Lean on management and innovation

TIFA, the training institute of the Belgian Federal Authority, developed a training programme to develop skills in management techniques and tools. Its main concern was to develop a programme directly **applicable** to the workplace, resulting in a clear **impact** on the institution. The programme is targeted at management support, middle management and project leaders. It focuses on management techniques and tools such as work measurement, internal control, change management, process and project management, management agreements, quality management, and dashboards.

For every management technique the programme offers three kinds of training: Self Service, Co-lab and Academy. The Self Service is an open webpage with reference material including articles, checklists, videos, useful links, exercises and cases selected by the programme's trainers. The Co-Labs are interactive one- or two-day training courses that already have the basics of management techniques. The aim is foremost to learn from each other through cases, exercises, feedback and hands-on tips. In order to participate in a Colab, an entry test is required to prove you are capable of managing the Self-service material. The Academy offers expert support on the occasion of a concrete project. Project teams can present their project related to a determined management technique.

Box 4.3. Training senior and middle management in Estonia and Belgium *(continued)*

Once selected, a full year's training and intensive support are provided. The result: a project on management techniques implemented in your own organisation.

An example of such an Academy offered by TIFA is the Lean Academy, where participants themselves choose the offer and compose their trajectory according to their experience and needs.

The supervisors and trainers are themselves federal civil servants embedded in the daily practice. They pass on the available knowledge to the trainees. Source: Belgium PEM delegate

Source: Information from the Estonian and Belgian PEM delegates.

Using these examples as inspiration, the DNSC and *Laboratorio* could integrate innovation as a key component of a training programme for Public Managers. This programme would likely benefit both members of the SES and members of the middle management layers, either jointly or in different versions, and would need to take a blended approach to learning, relying heavily on experiential learning and reflection, case studies and hands-on training (see Chapter 1 for discussion of innovation training).

A first step would be to carry out an in-depth analysis of training needs that would build on the analysis made during this review process, collect more information about the organisational culture in the different ministries (see Chapter 2, section on organisational culture), different leadership styles, organisational strategy and individual training needs. This training needs analysis, and the subsequent training programme for managers, could be conducted by the DNSC with support from the Lab, which seems to be in the best position to identify trainers and eventually to jointly provide the training programme.

A specific module on leadership for innovation could also be integrated within regular leadership training. For example, the challenges for the DNSC in 2016 (as highlighted in the *Balance de Gestion Integral* 2015 published by DIPRES) include the implementation of a *Modelo de Desarrollo de Directivos Públicos* and design and implement a pilot system of training for public leadership. These training courses include leadership training, networking and trust building, and leadership for innovation could be developed as an additional module in the training programme.

As important as it is to develop senior leaders, middle managers and direct supervisors have a potentially greater motivational impact on their employees, and the quality of this relationship is fundamental for motivating staff and engaging their creativity. Furthermore, middle managers should be considered as potential senior managers in development. Some of mechanisms which aim at supporting bottom-up innovation processes like *Experimenta*, could also be used to support middle managers by creating an additional space for them to meet, develop their skills and discuss the challenges they face. In this way both Belgium and Estonia align middle management training and development with their senior leadership programmes to ensure they are both aligned with each other.

Recognising that learning is not confined to formal training, networks for managers may also be effective to help managers translate the Presidential innovation mandate into concrete innovations at institutional level. While the Network of innovators seems to be a natural space for this, it could be anticipated to have a special "sub-network" for managers. For example, Denmark has a dedicated innovation-oriented network for managers, which also includes a confidential space to share the difficult parts of innovation processes, and facilitate open discussions about possible solutions.

Since innovation is a constant learning process, managers of innovation projects could benefit from support and coaching at various moments of a project's lifecycle. Some public agencies in Chile's central government have already set up innovation units at institutional level which could play a role in supporting middle managers. At the moment, the OECD is aware of six ministries which have created their own innovation units: Public Works, Housing and Urban Development, SEGPRES, Economy, Finance and Interior. Some institutions at lower levels have also created such units; this is the case of the Gendarmería, Fondo de Solidaridad e Inversion Social (FOSIS), Agriculture and Livestock Service, Council for Transparency, CODELCO, Subsecretary of Regional Development and Sub-secretariat of Transportation.

There could be an opportunity to bring these units together to share practices and examples of the successes and difficulties of the interactions they have with managers and to pool resources, knowledge and skills related to innovation-oriented management coaching.

Fourth, some OECD countries integrate innovation in performance assessment criteria. Developing performance objectives that encourage safe risk taking or experimentation, or that reward innovation oriented behaviour may be some of the ways to improve motivation to innovate in an organisation, linking innovation to career advancement. Canada for example has included innovation in its Key Leadership Competency profile, and leaders are assessed for promoting innovation and guiding change.

Box 4.4. Canada's Key Leadership Competencies

Leaders play a pivotal role in creating and sustaining a modern, connected and high-performing public service that is ethical, professional and non-partisan.

The Key Leadership Competencies define the behaviours expected of leaders in Canada's Public Service in six areas: Create Vision and Strategy, Mobilize People, Uphold Integrity and Respect, Collaborate with Partners and Stakeholders, Promote Innovation and Guide Change, and Achieve Results. This competency profile serves as the basis for selection, learning and development, performance and talent management of executives and other senior leaders. At the beginning of the fiscal year, managers of executives set performance and behavioural expectations, based on the Government of Canada's and departmental priorities and expected demonstration of the Key Leadership Competencies. At the end of the fiscal year, managers are required to assess results achieved by the executive including how the executive promoted innovation.

Among other things, managers must consider how the executive demonstrated the courage and resilience to challenge convention; created an environment that supported bold thinking, Experimentation and intelligent risk taking; used setbacks as a valuable source of insight and learning; took change in their stride, aligned and adjusted milestones and targets to maintain forward momentum. The year-end assessment of executives serves as the basis for performance rating decisions and performance-based compensation.

Sources: information from the Canadian PEM delegate; Tresury Board Canada, https://www.canada.ca/en/treasury-board-secretariat/services/professional-development/key-leadership-competency-profile/examples-effective-ineffective-behaviours.html.

Conclusions and recommendations

On creating a vision and mainstreaming innovation across the whole the Chilean administration

- Senior Leaders play an integral role in setting, communicating and valuing innovation in their organisation, in effect creating the opportunity and space for innovation. Chile could consider developing a whole-of-government vision or agenda for public sector innovation, to build a common narrative for public leaders with which to align their actions. To be effective, the vision should incorporate the input and views of a wide set of public leaders, be principles-based and aspirational, and leave room for public leaders' own innovation in their implementation of its principle. It should also link into current and ongoing work on public service development.

On how leaders can create space and support for more innovation in the civil service

- The ADP system, managed by the DNSC, is a recognised best practice in competency-based ADP recruitment and ensures a high level of capacity in Chile's public leadership, and which should be further strengthened by the implementation of Law No. 20.955/2016. The existence of innovation and flexibility in the competency framework provides an opportunity to discuss and further refine this competency, towards more clearly defining what this means in practice. Afterwards, this can be reinforced through performance management and development.
- The development of stable and sustainable leadership with the right skills to manage innovation should not be overlooked when considering the sustainability of high turnover of senior managers who only stay in their positions on average two to three years makes it even more important to consider middle managers as key elements in supporting bottom-up innovation. The DNSC and the lab should involve more middle managers in innovation activities, for example in the preparation of guidelines for recruitment, performance assessment or training. A short-term mobility period in a different public organisation could be used to make managers more aware of PSI, and also to facilitate transferring skills from one team to another.
- While the current plans of the Innovation Agenda for Public Managers only anticipates the involvement of managers in the Innovators' network, the design of a training programme for senior and middle public managers could provide a stronger contribution and sign of commitment to the development of leadership skills for innovation. Such a training programme could be developed by the *Laboratorio* and the DNSC.
- A senior leader's network can provide a forum to share practical experiences about creating space for innovation within organisations, and also to discuss shared innovation issues and challenges. It can also be used as a space to collaborate on demonstration projects that explore and typify new ways of working, and can contribute to cross-agency initiatives to foster a culture of innovation.

Notes

1 www.serviciocivil.gob.cl/convenios-orientaciones

2 www.anzsog.edu.au/executive-workshops/executive-workshops/delivering-better-outcomes-leading-public-sector-innovation

References

Beauchamp, Glenys (2015), "Innovation Month and Supporting Innovation Across the APS", Australian Government, Public Sector Innovation, http://innovation.govspace.gov.au/2015/07/06/innovation-month-and-supporting-innovation-across-the-aps/.

Hazlehurst, D. (30 March 2016), "Sixth Meeting of the Innovation Champions Group", Australian Government, Public Sector Innovation, http://innovation.govspace.gov.au/2016/03/30/sixth-meeting-of-the-innovation-champions-group/.

Ministerio de Hacienda (2015), Balance de Gestión Integral, Año 2015, Dirección Nacional del Servicio Civil, available in http://www.dipres.gob.cl/595/articles-147110_doc_pdf.pdf.

OECD (2017), Fostering Innovation in the Public Sector, OECD Publishing, Paris. http://dx.doi.org/10.1787/9789264270879-en.

OECD (2016), *Engaging Public Employees for a High-Performing Civil Service*, OECD Public Governance Reviews, OECD Publishing, Paris, http://dx.doi.org/10.1787/9789264267190-en

OECD (2015), *The Innovation Imperative in the Public Sector: Setting an Agenda for Action*, OECD Publishing, Paris, http://dx.doi.org/10.1787/9789264236561-en.

Roberts, A. (15 February 2016), "Innovation Behaviours for the Public Service – beta version", Australian Government, Public Sector Innovation, http://innovation.govspace.gov.au/2016/02/15/innovation-behaviours-for-the-public-service-beta-version/.

Tresury Board Canada, Key Leadership Competency profile and examples of effective and ineffective behaviours, https://www.canada.ca/en/treasury-board-secretariat/services/professional-development/key-leadership-competency-profile/examples-effective-ineffective-behaviours.html.

Chapter 5.

Creating an innovation-ready public sector workforce in Chile

This chapter takes stock of the efforts underway in Chile's public sector to build innovation capabilities in the public sector and charts a way forward. Public sector innovation involves different areas that have complex interrelations. As such, fostering innovation requires developing parallel and complementary approaches by different actors. In this sense, this section suggests a path forward for three of the institutions that play a major role in public sector innovation: the Laboratorio de Gobierno, whose mandate is to foster public sector innovation capabilities across government; the National Civil Service Directorate, for its central role in the recruitment, development and management of civil servants; and all public leaders and managers in the Chilean civil service, who are central to implementing change and unleashing the potential of innovators.

Enabling and supporting public sector innovation by addressing the workforce's abilities, motivations and opportunities to innovate is emerging as a current and future priority in many OECD countries. Yet the evidence base of what works and how this can be achieved is still underdeveloped. This report has identified some emerging practices designed to contribute to a more innovation-ready public sector workforce in Chile and abroad. Looking forward, careful attention will be required to implement, sustain, monitor and evaluate these practices with a view to developing guidance for policy makers when planning activities intended to improve the place of innovation in the public sector and make it systematic.

As suggested by the framework Abilities – Motivation – Opportunities, public sector innovation involves different areas that have complex interrelations, going from recruitment to development of civil servants, from innovation awards to networks of innovators, from strengthening a collaborative organisational culture to developing the capacity to lead innovation. As such, fostering innovation requires developing parallel and complementary approaches by different actors. In this sense, this section presents a number of conclusions for three of the primary actors that play a major role in public sector innovation: the *Laboratorio*, whose mandate is to foster PSI across government; the DNCS, for its central role in the recruitment, development and management of civil servants; and all public leaders and managers in the Chilean civil service, who are central to implementing change and unleashing the potential of innovators.

The Government of Chile: From accelerating to institutionalising public sector innovation

Innovation in the public sector does not happen on its own; central government has an important role in creating an environment conducive to innovation and promotes the enabling condition for civil servants to come up with novel solutions. As a transformation process, innovation requires mastering specific tools and methods that public servants can use to navigate from challenge discovery and ideas generation to final implementation. The methods and process are in constant flux and evolve as the practice extends to various policy domains. To succeed in achieving innovation, governments need to make innovation the rule not the exception, creating permanent conduits to embed these practices in public sector organisations' operating systems. The *Laboratorio* is doing a good job in creating greater awareness of the potential of the use of innovation to change policy and service delivery in Chile, and acting as a demonstrator of the positive impact of innovation in the everyday life of citizens. In moving, it would be advisable for the Chilean government to take stock of the many innovation initiatives across government and strengthen efforts to further disseminate lessons and take actions to bring innovative approaches in the DNA of public sector agencies into the mainstream. In its efforts to institutionalise innovation in public sector policies and practices, the government of Chile might consider the following actions:

- Reflect on the opportunity for a whole-of-government public sector innovation strategy identifying key cross-government objectives linked up with the President's Agenda; supporting greater experimentation and setting up the conditions for it; creating incentives for the use of innovative methods and tools to solve public challenges.
- Make sure an appropriate high-level body is in place to ensure the co-ordination of this strategy and participation from the top level of government organisations.

This body will need to ensure continuous prioritisation, co-ordination of action and sharing of learnings across the administration. It could also be given the task of preparing the public sector innovation strategy. This high-level body should be closely connected with the government agenda and draw its membership from key government actors in this field.

- Position the *Laboratorio* as the Government Innovation unit and develop its capacity to closely connect its activities to the Government's agenda and policy priorities; to develop a compelling narrative communicating its successes inside government; to effectively support innovation units and projects across government in using innovative methods and tools.

Laboratorio de Gobierno: Providing civil servants with opportunities to innovate

The innovation imperative has seen the proliferation of different forms of innovation units, teams and organisation across OECD governments, emerging as the institutional expression of the will and need to embed innovation into the public sector's machinery and ways of working. Generally, these units bring together a diversity of skill sets and approaches from a wide variety of disciplines, ranging from public policy to anthropology and design (OECD, 2017 forthcoming). Often the objective of these units or teams is to find solutions to problems that resist traditional public sector approaches by gaining a deeper level of understanding of the issue. However their activities also tend to include training courses and workshops for civil servants as well as advice or guidance for ministries and agencies. Increasingly, these teams or units are also expected to promote an innovation culture in their respective areas of work and spread the use of new methods, processes and approaches to rethink how public organisations operate.

In this way, Chile's *Laboratorio de Gobierno* can be positioned within a new movement of government intervention, which tends to have an impact on civil servants' abilities, motivations and opportunities to innovate. Taking the analyses in the three main chapters, a number of themes emerge which point towards a role for the *Laboratorio* to promote each of the three themes:

- **Abilities**: In addition to regular training programmes, the *Laboratorio* has created the programme *Experimenta* to develop innovation skills in a selected group of public employees. This programme has great potential to develop civil servants' skills for innovation through a learning-by-doing approach. However, the programme is new and itself in many ways and experiment. Being able to monitor the programme's implementation and measure its impact will be crucial to demonstrate its value and to identify shortcomings and make adjustments. Also, documenting the experience and creating ways for sharing the results more widely would help diffuse the benefits and lessons and generate interest among larger group of civil servants.
  - Recommendation: Take steps to develop a methodology to monitor and measure the impact of *Experimenta* at the outset and after the programme has ended. Identify ways to diffuse this approach to larger groups of civil servants beyond participants
- **Motivation**: The network of innovators is an important tool to recognise support and motivate innovators, yet it still needs to move from its initial roll-out phase to demonstrating its value to its members. Activities of the Public Innovators Network could include learning activities, for example national events (like the

National Summit of Public Innovators scheduled to take place in April 2017) or smaller workshops (like the launching of the network in November 2015), oriented towards specific skills development and knowledge sharing. Finally, the network could be used to promote the implementation of innovations directly inspired by examples from the Chilean public administration. For example, a mentoring scheme could bring together current and future innovators.

- Recommendation: Set up clear "rules of engagement" between the *Laboratorio* and the members of the networks, detailing responsibilities, modes of participation and expected benefits for its members. These rules should clearly identify the role of the *Laboratorio* in supporting this network and how its activities should be realigned to support the network members. These rules could be defined in a collaborative way engaging the network with the *Laboratorio* in a co-creation exercise. The potential directions of the Public Innovators Community raise questions about the role of the *Laboratorio* in supporting this network: what should be the scope of its activities vis-à-vis the network members (e.g. ownership) and how to ensure the *Laboratorio* continues to support it as the network grows

- **Opportunities**: The *Laboratorio* convenes civil servants interested in innovation and should play a contributing role to higher-level discussions on the development of a common vision, and a cadre of ADP with the skills and motivations to ensure their public employees are given opportunities to innovate.
  - Recommendation: Ensure the *Laboratorio* is equipped to provide substantive input in the formation of a whole-of-government innovation agenda building on the insights and knowledge built through learning by doing and training programmes. Set up a mechanism to systematically disseminate lessons and results from innovative intervention and training outwards but also upwards to leaders at the highest levels.

As the *Laboratorio* takes stock of its potential role in contributing to the Abilities, Motivations and Opportunities of civil servants to innovate, the Government of Chile also needs to ask what kind of lab is required to deliver on these expectations. The way the *Laboratorio* is currently functioning to build the capabilities of civil servants to innovate is similar to other government labs in OECD countries:

- The US OPM Innovation Lab serves the entire federal government with a focus on building innovative design capabilities in the workforce and do so by partnerships with institutions to allow public employees to learn innovative design capabilities through experience (Box 5.1).
- DesignGov in the Australian federal government, which was an 18-month pilot of a whole-of-government innovation lab, had a mission to "build innovation capability in the APS and provide for better outcomes through applied problem solving, including at the interface between the APS, other jurisdictions and providers, and the users of services." This was implemented through streams of actives focusing for example on capability building among civil servants through design-led approaches (Box 5.2).

A majority of these "classical government laboratory examples" often do work on a project basis, where labs partner with certain departments to design, develop and implement innovative interventions to increase value for citizens or the user. That said, these institutions are increasingly exploring how they can diffuse innovation more widely across government, as opposed to targeted innovation projects. This means integrating innovation methods and innovative working in everyday routines, in policy-making considerations, and when developing or re-evaluating how to deliver services to citizens and business.

Some government labs are tackling this challenge by creating stronger linkages with the executive. The Canadian Central Innovation Hub for example has experienced a shift from project support to positioning in the delivery and results function at the centre of government, providing a stronger case for using different tools as part of civil servants' mainstream thinking when developing policies and services and delivering results for citizens (Box 5.3).

Other labs such as MindLab in Denmark have evolved considerably over time to a model which is based fully on incorporating a culture of innovation among the leader and within the administration. In this sense, the Lab sets this as its main goal, and then considers what type of interventions can achieve it, which may vary (Box 5.4). This purpose-based organisational model was built up over time and was highly dependent on the track record it formed over the years and the trust it built up with the owners of the Lab. MindLab is beginning to track and measure how its interventions are leading to behavioural and cultural changes within the administration via a qualitative approach called "signs of success" (Box 5.4).

The French laboratory Futurs Publics is working closely to sustain diffusion of innovative methods and approaches across the public sector. This is done through funding programmes such as the "Territorial Innovation Laboratories" which aims at adapting, developing and diffusing new collaborative ways of working with local agencies of central government bodies. This model links financing mechanisms (as part of the Future Investment Programme) to strengthen local office capabilities to operate as innovation laboratories.

The *Laboratorio* has achieved a first stage of development, where its main focus is giving civil servants the opportunity to learn about and use innovative methods and tools via a controlled environment (i.e. first generation in terms of the MindLab classification). The *Laboratorio* will now need to consider how its role will evolve and mature as an institution over time, in particular as it moves from promoting an understanding of new methods and skills to helping public sector organisations to incorporate them in their operating environment. This will require the *Laboratorio:*

- to re-evaluate its working environment and to assess how its mission needs to evolve to continue promoting an organisational culture that values innovation
- to encourage stronger linkages with innovation units in other ministries or agencies where they exist and/or support innovators in their efforts to develop innovation capacities in their own organisations.

As the role and purpose of the *Laboratorio* evolves, it will also be important to align their own skills and capacities with the new and increasing roles they take on as an institution and the new missions they set. This relates both to the immediate new missions and programmes the *Laboratorio* is increasingly taking on (i.e. *Experimenta*), but also to the evolving role and mission the *Laboratorio* will take on over time. As seen in the evolution of MindLab, capabilities needed in the Lab during its first generation did not necessarily match the staff profiles needed in the third generation of the Lab. These profiles now include a greater emphasis on communication skills and staff with senior advisory capacities in order to work with the owning partners to align and determine the scope of the projects. While the first generation of MindLab focused heavily on recruiting staff with design skills, experience has shown that staff with public sector experience, and those who know how to navigate and advise public sector leaders can be beneficial. To this end, the *Laboratorio* could consider:

- ensuring the *Laboratorio*'s own skills and capacities are aligned with the current expanding missions and programmes (i.e. in staff profiles and resources)
- planning for the skills and capacities the *Laboratorio* will require to meet the Lab's new model and mission, which will undoubtedly evolve over time
- identifying the tools and mechanisms to promote the development and diffusion of lab capabilities across the public sector.

On a shorter term basis, the *Laboratorio* could also consider developing and presenting qualitative measures of their success to date (similar to the Canadian and Danish examples) as a communication tool to demonstrate the successes of the *Laboratorio* so far, and also as a way to enhance understanding of the Lab's activities among civil servants. The activity in itself is also a good starting point to discuss what success would be like, and what qualitative signs the *Laboratorio* would look for to demonstrate that their interventions are successful and are demonstrating impact.

This may require giving thought to the governance of the *Laboratorio* now and in the future to ensure that it is fit for the purpose, as evolutions in the lab's role may suggest other models. Questions that arise may include the following:

- The rationale behind the formation of the board was to select strategic, cross-cutting ministries to own the direction of the Lab. However, unlike the governance of MindLab in the Danish government, the owners are not the clients of the Lab, but instead are responsible for making decisions on its strategic orientations and goals. While this positioning allowed the *Laboratorio* to have greater influence across government and enjoy a greater level of collaboration, especially during its early years, consideration should be given to the extent to which this model enables rapid decision taking and capacity to swiftly change direction when needed.
- The participation of civil society is a unique feature in the Board's governance, demonstrates government openness in agenda setting and provides external legitimacy to *Laboratorio* actions. Yet, consideration should be given to whether a larger non-governmental membership well-suited to hosting cross-government strategic thinking, and how to account for unequal levels of accountability in relation to the board deliberations, especially when it comes to pioneering initiatives in politically-sensitive areas.

Box 5.1. The United States Office for Personnel and Management (OPM) Innovation Lab

The US OMP Innovation Lab serves the entire federal government with a focus on building innovative design capabilities in the workforce. The Lab is currently governed by the internal management structures of OMP and is situated in the Human Resource Solutions division, which provides human resources products and services to the entire Federal Government and houses the Center for Leadership Development among others. For the first two years of inception, the Lab was funded by OMP and was an institution directly for OMP's use.

Starting in January 2015, the Lab moved to a cost-recovery model, where they now partner institutions government-wide to carry out projects on a pay-for-services basis. The number of full-time staff has grown from about 4-5 OMP at inception to now over 15, with this number still increasing. The team is diverse from private and public sector but mainly have design backgrounds.

The Lab guides its activities with the mission of Lead/Do/Teach, engaging in projects with a variety of government institutions as well as providing customised training courses and information sessions. Some of the ongoing projects with partner institutions include redesigning the public portal advertising government jobs (USA jobs), two projects with Veteran Affairs, and a cross-cutting project in OPM to build capacity across government for customer service, which is a cross-priority goal set at the highest level of government.

In terms of evaluating the impact and results of their work and projects, the Lab looks for concrete results such as cost savings and partnerships formed or numbers of people reached. For example, the Lab has a dedicated staff to decide on performance measures for certain projects, in collaboration with project partners. For broader workshops and training courses, the Lab also measures customer satisfaction and gains feedback through surveys at the end of classes.

Source: Interview with US OPM Innovation Lab.

Box 5.2. Australia: DesignGov

DesignGov was an 18-month pilot of a whole-of-government innovation lab that ran from July 2012 to December 2013. The pilot was endorsed by the Portfolio Secretaries of the Australian Public Service (APS) and was run from the Industry Department with support (active or in-kind) from a number of other government agencies.

The mission of DesignGov, as set out in its Charter document, was to "inspire creativity, innovation and a more citizen-centric approach through consultation, collaboration and co-design." It was to "build innovation capability in the APS and provide for better outcomes through applied problem solving, including at the interface between the APS, other jurisdictions and providers, and the users of services".

DesignGov was overseen by a high-level Board and, through it, reported to the Portfolio Secretaries. It had four streams of activity including:

- demonstration projects
- engagement, education and awareness
- capability building, methodologies and tools
- operating framework, governance and reporting.

Box 5.2. Australia: DesignGov *(continued)*

DesignGov's major demonstration project was "how might we dramatically improve business/government interactions" and involved a series of workshops, interviews with businesses, public servants and intermediaries and survey response. Using a design-led approach, DesignGov published a series of findings and recommendations about how interaction between business and government could be reframed and improved. Initial work was done on developing prototypes of the five recommendation areas.

The DesignGov experiment was closed in December 2013 at the end of the trial period.

Source: DesignGov, https://innovation.govspace.gov.au/category/designgov.

Box 5.3. The Canadian Central Innovation Hub

The Central Innovation Hub has been running for about a year and a half and is located in the Privy Council Office, which is the department for the Prime Minister and serves as the main policy space for the Prime Minister's Office. The Hub was established to enhance the knowledge of innovative policy approaches and instruments and directly support the development and implementation of innovative programmes and services throughout government. The Hub will soon move to the results and delivery function within the Privy Council Office, allowing its work to be more closely connected with the top priority areas of government and importantly helping emphasise that innovation and using different tools should be part of civil servants' mainstream thinking when delivering results for citizens.

The Hub's objectives are closely aligned with several of the Government's commitments and can serve as a key tool for advancing this agenda. For example, the Government has emphasised the importance of improving implementation through better linkages between policy advice, programme design and delivery; more open and transparent policy-making; innovative policy tools and financing instruments; programme experimentation; and evidence-based policy development.

The Hub currently has three core areas of practice: behavioural insights, data and design. Cutting across these core areas is "Policy development to spark innovation" where the Hub works to provide the policy rationale and create space for the government to pursue more innovative approaches in policy development and implementation.

Through these areas of practice, the Hub has oriented its work to incorporate three horizontal objectives to act as:

- **a resource** – providing easy access to information on best practices and new tools, approaches, and techniques
- **a connector** – establishing networks and partnerships between project leads and resources to accelerate departmental work
- **an innovation catalyst** – working with department to identify and support projects with potential for large scale impact and assess and document results in order to draw system-wide benefits from lessons learned.

In concrete terms the Hub works with agencies on specific projects – whether they are general activities (such as two-hour informational workshops on applying a tool in participants' work) to nine-month projects working with a department. The Hub team has six full-time staff with two to three rotating on a project basis.

Box 5.3. The Canadian Central Innovation Hub *(continued)*

After its first year in operation, the Hub produced an evaluation report which focused on early innovation results and efforts made (see below). While the Hub intends to develop more specific metrics to evaluate its impact, the visualisation of early indicators of success can prove a useful communication tool to use across government.

Early indicators of success

Source: The Government of Canada, "The Innovation Hub", www.pco-bcp.gc.ca/docs/innovation/rpt3/docs/rpt-eng.pdf.

Box 5.4. MindLab Denmark

MindLab is co-owned and funded by four public organisations: the Ministry of Business and Growth, the Ministry of Education, the Ministry of Employment and the Odense Municipality. The Lab serves these institutions by developing projects with them that fulfil the Labs main purpose: to incorporate a culture of innovation among the leaders and within the administration. While needs across MindLabs' owning partners vary, strategic orientation of the Lab is given by the management board which consists of the Permanent Secretaries of the four organisations. This has recently taken the form of "ambition papers", which are developed by the owning partners and by MindLab, and seek to set the ambition for the lab over a three-year period, including what changes are hoped for, rather than specific KPIs. These ambition papers also form the basis for strategic discussion over MindLab's project selection over the next three to six months, where the projects also need to take into account the ambition to affect citizens. MindLab helps facilitates specific projects, but the project 'owners' are the relevant agency, as they are the ones making the change.

The current model of MindLab – which is purpose driven – has evolved considerably since the Lab's inception. The evolution of the Lab could be thought of in the following manner:

- **1st generation** of MindLab focused on specific methods and tools for innovation
- **2nd generation** of MindLab was user-centred and design focused, taking a wider view of the needs of the citizen

Box 5.4. MindLab Denmark *(continued)*

- **3rd generation (current model)** of MindLab is purpose based, and focuses on researching and developing the cultural behaviour needed to diffuse innovation more broadly within the administration (it concerns trying to pioneer a culture change). This current approach is about identifying the behaviours and identifying enabling conditions that will help contribute to achieving the Lab's purpose - to incorporate a culture of innovation within the administration. During this current generation, many different staff profiles were recruited to meet the Lab's new model and mission, including philosophers, journalists, and staff with senior advisory capacities so as to work with the owning partners to align and determine the scope of the projects.

This generational evolution has meant a change in focus from very specific interventions to increasingly experimental and dynamic interventions that are tied to the specific project and the purpose at hand.

During this third phase, examples of types of initiatives that were developed to contribute to the purpose include an event with civil servants which looked at the barriers and opportunities for innovation from the perspective of the civil servants, and then also with managers, including discussion on how to overcome these obstacles. Another intervention agreed on by the owning partners of the Lab was a public start-up project to shorten the time normally taken to identify a problem and propose a solution. The project brought together a group of people for two weeks to understand a major problem, and then provide a prototype of possible solutions. In both cases, the purpose is determined, and then the type of intervention is developed. This type of approach requires considerable trust by the owners of the Lab, which is built up over time. The Lab staff members are also open about failures, and are good at communicating and convincing people of the value of projects.

Evaluating the impact of interventions – signs of success

MindLab is working on a more qualitative approach to measure the impact of their interventions which is called "signs of success". Success of the Lab's work is measured by 3 variables:

1. **returning customers** – the clients and people involved in projects/seminars like the work of MindLab and are happy with it
2. **a project takes on a different approach to the citizen** – the intervention of MindLab means that the project owners take on a new or changed approach to the citizen during the process of the project
3. **the Lab sees some of the behaviour changes that demonstrate that innovation is incorporated into the culture** – to be able to see the methods within the administration demonstrated.

"Signs of success" has been running for four months, and are collected on a weekly basis. Now MindLab is seeking to see patterns, and to scale up. The aim of the tool is to try to understand the enabling conditions – what makes this possible – and to find patterns to scale up.

Source: information provided to the OECD from MindLab, Denmark.

Using the tools available to the DNSC to promote a more innovative civil service

The DNSC has been a lead player in the improvement of human resource management and development across the Chilean public sector: the Manual for recruitment, the *PMG Capacitacion*, or the System of *Alta Direction Publica* are some examples of its efforts towards a more professional and strategic civil service. In this regard, the DNSC must continue to be a key player in capacity building for public sector innovation. While the *Funciona!* awards are the most visible aspect of DNSC's support for public sector innovation, the DNSC influences many other elements that contribute to improving abilities for innovation, motivating innovators and creating the right opportunities.

The DNSC's role in supporting public sector innovation will become even more central as its overall role in HR management and Senior Civil Service is strengthened by the new Law 20.955/2016. This means great authority in setting common standards in central areas such as the recruitment of all civil servants and the development and training programmes run in individual services, and common standards for performance management, including at the most senior levels. As the DNSC works out the details of the implementation process, great opportunities exist to include innovation capacity building elements into the tools and processes that will be established. With this in mind, the following recommendations should be considered.

Abilities

- Recruitment: Building a skilled workforce is the first step to supporting public sector innovation in a sustainable way. The DNSC produces a number of tools such as the *Plan de Asesorias en Recluatmiento y seleccion* and the *Manual Seleccion de Personas en servicios publicos*, to guide individual entities in their recruitment processes. As the DNSC begins to implement the new law, it would be a good time to review these tools to identify ways they could be used to support more innovation-oriented recruitment and selection.
  - Recommendation: Undertake an innovation-oriented review of the tools available to standardise recruitment processes in light of the new legislation. Involve a range of experts, including, for example, staff at the *Laboratorio*, HR professionals, and recruiting managers from ministries and agencies with experience in innovation.
- Development: In parallel with recruitment for innovation, developing skills for innovation in Chile can be done through learning and development programmes. In this sense, the next three-year training strategy (prepared by the DNSC) could be used to raise awareness about skills for innovation and facilitate the alignment of institutional training plans with the government-wide innovation mandate.
  - Recommendation: Include elements of innovation training in the next three-year training strategy. Work with the *Laboratorio* to set quality standards for innovation training and ensure systems are in place to evaluate and adjust training to meet demand. Include specific focus on training and incentives for middle management. Leverage existing tools such as Sispubli to collect additional data on the development of skills for innovation, and *Convenio Marcos* to select training providers.

- Mobility: Giving employees and leaders opportunities to work outside their home organisation can offer opportunities to develop new insights and build new skills by giving the individual a more horizontal understanding of policy issues and allowing them to look at things from outside their sector perspective. Mobility can also increase the exchange of ideas and problem solving approaches.
  - Recommendation: develop a form of innovation internship programme that can enable employees from one organisation to move temporarily to another to work on specific innovation projects. This could include working in the *Laboratorio* for 6-12 months on specific projects. This programme should be managed from the DNSC so as to enable appropriate matching of skills to needs.

Motivation:

- In Chile, the organisational culture is often perceived as non-supportive of innovation. In this regard, the first thing to help achieve a better understanding of the influence of the organisational culture in the motivation of civil servants to innovate would be to measure it better.
  - Recommendation: explore opportunities to develop a survey module with questions about the perception of civil servants on their ability and motivation to innovate in their work, and also about the opportunities that they have to implement to contribute and implement their ideas. This could build on existing surveys but should be broad in scope, to include a range of institutions in order to benchmark. Ensure a broad level of engagement in the development and dissemination of results.
- While Chile has developed a number of innovation contests and awards since the 1990's, there is space to scale up the impact of shortlisted and award-winning innovations.
  - Recommendation: Use the *Funciona!* award to collect and share innovation in ways that support inspiration and eventual replication. This could include building an online database of all winners and shortlisted innovations to provide visibility and inspiration to other agencies. It can also include specific programmes aimed at replicating successful innovation in other services or regions.

Opportunity:

- The Senior Civil Service (SADP), managed by the DNSC, is a recognised best practice in competency-based recruitment and ensures a high level of capacity in Chile's public leadership. The existence of innovation and flexibility in the competency framework provides an opportunity to discuss and further refine this competency, towards more clearly defining what this means in practice. This is all the more important today, given the planned expansion of the performance management system under the new law.
  - Recommendation: Develop a network of senior level innovators to support the development of guidelines on innovation-oriented leadership, through a process of broad consultation. Use these guidelines to reinforce the innovation competency already included in the SADP recruitment system throughout the

careers of SES through regular performance management and leadership development. This network may be based on the high-level innovation committee recommended earlier in this chapter.

Towards a more innovative public management in Chile: A role for every public manager.

Public managers play the most important role in setting, communicating and valuing innovation in their organisation, and in creating the opportunity and space for innovation. They are in a position where they can influence the organisational culture and values, and under certain conditions they can have a positive effect on performance, motivation and satisfaction of their teams (Orazi et al., 2013). As such, the *Laboratorio* and the DNSC will only create an effect through the role played by public managers and their commitment towards innovation.

Abilities and Motivation: Building a skilled cadre of middle managers

- Building an innovation oriented culture and workforce relies greatly on the capacity of middle management – those who are directly responsible for designing teams, assigning work, giving feedback and maintaining a positive and open working environment in the face of complexity, ambiguity and great challenges. Their role is all the more important, given the relatively short time senior managers stay. Therefore, scaling up public sector innovation in the Chilean administration will require an active role of middle managers.
  - Recommendation to senior leaders: Set expectations for middle managers to adhere to certain innovation-oriented behaviour and ensure that innovation is included as a module in management training. Senior leaders should also create spaces for managers to exchange ideas openly and to feed their ideas up to the highest organisational levels. Senior managers should look at opportunities to set up and support innovation units within their institutions to support managers and other public employees. Finally, senior managers should find ways to reward middle managers who display innovative behaviour.

Opportunities: Creating a vision; building space; using multidisciplinary teams

- Senior Leaders play an integral role in setting, communicating and valuing innovation in their organisation, in effect creating the opportunity and space for innovation. Developing a whole-of-government vision or agenda for public sector innovation, as recommended at the beginning of this chapter, would help senior leaders to build a common narrative and language around innovation, to help guide and align their actions. To be effective, the vision should incorporate the input and views of a wide set of public leaders, be principles-based and aspirational, and leave room for public leaders' own innovation in their implementation of its principles.
  - Recommendation: Set up a group dedicated to championing innovation, consisting of a senior contact point in each public organisation across the administration, drawing lessons from the Australian Innovation Champions Group. This group can provide a forum to share practical experiences about creating space for innovation within organisations, and also to discuss shared

innovation issues and challenges. It can also be used as a space to collaborate on demonstration projects that explore and typify new ways of working, and can contribute to cross-agency initiatives to foster a culture of innovation. It can provide input into DNSC projects intended to improve recruitment, training and leadership. It can provide input into the development of vision/agenda on innovation and provide a conduit into each organisation for its implementation.

Looking forward: Next steps for researching the ability, motivation and opportunities for public sector innovation in Chile

This study has been exploratory and ground breaking: it is the first study of civil servants' skills and capacity to drive and implement public sector innovation in a national government. It contributes to the knowledge being generated on both Public Sector Innovation and on Civil Service Reform. As a first study, the focus was primarily on institutional mechanisms that govern employment and capacity building in Chile's public administration. The study focused far and wide, in order to try to incorporate as great a range of perspectives as possible. However there are limits to the breadth and the depth of this approach. In order to address these, the next steps in research into innovation capabilities could include the following:

Expanding the breadth of research by engaging more public employees

Through a combination of interviews and workshops, this project pulls together the views of over 300 key people involved in public sector innovation in Chile, from a wide range of institutions and at all levels of the organisational hierarchy. While this is a significant number, it is a small part of the total and not enough to establish a factual baseline of skills for innovation in Chile's public sector. Furthermore, it is a group that is probably not representative of the average public employee who previously had little involvement in public sector innovation.

One way to complement this breadth is to develop survey instruments. As discussed in Chapter 3, more and more countries are investing in employee surveys to get a deeper understanding of employee commitment, motivation, and their perceptions of their work environment. Questions related to innovation can be designed and structured in ways that enable a useful analysis across large populations. Indeed, most OECD countries conduct an employee survey across their entire employee populations, resulting in hundreds of thousands of responses across every ministry and agency. This provides rich data to benchmark employees' perception of their abilities, motivation and opportunities to innovate.

Box 3.3 in Chapter 3 includes a sample of the innovation questions asked by Ireland, the UK and the US. Chile could develop a survey that incorporates similar questions to get a snapshot of the actual baseline. Box 2.3 in Chapter 2 includes the discussion of a different survey instrument that was piloted to understand the perception of a person's own skills, their support from their managers, and their organisation's readiness. Elements of these could also be included in a survey. The design and analysis of such a survey could first take place in a number of organisations as pilots, in order to ensure that the questions are clear and collect data as expected.

Depending on the question asked, the survey could provide significant insight into providing information for capacity building for public sector innovation. For example, it could help to identify organisations which score high, to discover good practices that could be shared and scaled. It could also be used to better understand which groups of employees (e.g. level of hierarchy, age, function, etc.) require which kinds of support.

Going deeper: looking at innovation skills and processes in key organisations

A second approach would be to go deeper into specific institutions that are interested in setting up a partnership with the *Laboratorio* for a closer look at their own management structures. One of the findings of this review is that the management practices of individual agencies have a significant impact on the abilities, motivations of public employees and the opportunities available to them.

A follow-up project to this review could be to conduct a similar approach within specific organisations, employing a range of methodologies. Surveys such as the one piloted in Box 2.3 could be used in various departments of the organisation. Interviews and focus groups could be conducted with senior management, HR professionals, middle managers and employees at the frontlines. This would enable an understanding of the complexities inherent in organisational management in Chile's public administration.

Case studies could be accompanied by specific training seminars to understand associated behaviours and challenges in developing public sector innovation skills. This could be done in combination with *Experimenta*, for example, as a way to encourage greater effect beyond the participants.

Finally, Chile can take steps to extend the analysis beyond people, to look at other pieces of the puzzle such as the regulatory environment, budgeting tools, partnership opportunities, and how these can support or hinder innovation in the Chilean civil service. Work on specific cross-cutting issues (e.g. risk management) could also support better evidence into the existing barriers civil servants have to overcome to build innovative capabilities.

References

DesignGov, https://innovation.govspace.gov.au/category/designgov.

OECD (2017, forthcoming), Core skills for public sector innovation: a model of skills to promote and enable innovation in public sector organisations.

The Government of Canada, "The Innovation Hub", www.pco-bcp.gc.ca/docs/innovation/rpt3/docs/rpt-eng.pdf.

ORGANISATION FOR ECONOMIC CO-OPERATION AND DEVELOPMENT

The OECD is a unique forum where governments work together to address the economic, social and environmental challenges of globalisation. The OECD is also at the forefront of efforts to understand and to help governments respond to new developments and concerns, such as corporate governance, the information economy and the challenges of an ageing population. The Organisation provides a setting where governments can compare policy experiences, seek answers to common problems, identify good practice and work to co-ordinate domestic and international policies.

The OECD member countries are: Australia, Austria, Belgium, Canada, Chile, the Czech Republic, Denmark, Estonia, Finland, France, Germany, Greece, Hungary, Iceland, Ireland, Israel, Italy, Japan, Korea, Latvia, Luxembourg, Mexico, the Netherlands, New Zealand, Norway, Poland, Portugal, the Slovak Republic, Slovenia, Spain, Sweden, Switzerland, Turkey, the United Kingdom and the United States. The European Union takes part in the work of the OECD.

OECD Publishing disseminates widely the results of the Organisation's statistics gathering and research on economic, social and environmental issues, as well as the conventions, guidelines and standards agreed by its members.

OECD PUBLISHING, 2, rue André-Pascal, 75775 PARIS CEDEX 16
(42 2017 21 1 P) ISBN 978-92-64-27327-6 – 2017

www.ingramcontent.com/pod-product-compliance
Lightning Source LLC
LaVergne TN
LVHW081410110826
845149LV00010B/1687

9789264273276